ucla undocumented immigrant students speak out

under**ground**under**grads**

Edited by Gabriela Madera, Angelo A. Mathay, Armin M. Najafi, Hector H. Saldívar, Stephanie Solis, Alyssa Jane M. Titong, Gaspar Rivera-Salgado, Janna Shadduck-Hernández, Kent Wong, Rebecca Frazier, and Julie Monroe

UCLA Center for Labor Research and Education
Los Angeles, California

Design by Wendell Pascual and Heather Henderson
Cover photo by Gisela M. Ramos

UCLA Center for Labor Research and Education, Los Angeles, 90095-1478
© 2008 by UCLA Center for Labor Research and Education
All rights reserved. Published 2008

Printed in the United States of America
Library of Congress Control Number: 2007941539
ISBN 978-0-89215-002-1

"The talented, dynamic young people captured in this book represent the hope for the future. They have done what society has asked of them: they have worked hard, studied hard, and have obtained educational success in spite of tremendous obstacles. Now it is society's turn to do the right thing. We need to pass the Dream Act, and we need to provide a path to citizenship to these young people and to millions of undocumented workers who contribute so much for the American dream."

– María Elena Durazo, Executive Secretary-Treasurer, Los Angeles County Federation of Labor

"These courageous undocumented students of UCLA are standing up for the rights of all undocumented people. Although immigrant workers throughout the generations have worked in the fields and built our cities, they have always been subjected to poor treatment and have been denied basic rights. The voices of these students should be heard in Sacramento, in Washington, DC, and they should inspire us all to work harder for full rights for all immigrants."

– Dolores Huerta, Cofounder, United Farm Workers of America

"Underground Undergrads *reveals an inconvenient truth behind the empty slogans of those who offer hate instead of compassion in the debate on undocumented migration. Around a third of those presently in undocumented status entered the country as minors in the company of adults. They are guilty of no transgression except obeying their parents. I'd like to think that the United States is not the sort of country that punishes children for the purported crimes of parents. After reading this book, surely no one can disagree that the students it profiles merit an immediate and unconditional amnesty. It is not only the right thing to do morally, it is the obvious move practically, for until the burden of undocumented status is lifted, these well-educated and ambitious students constitute a waste of valuable human capital that our country can ill afford to lose."*

– Douglas Massey, Professor of Sociology, Woodrow Wilson School, Princeton University

"In the midst of contentious debates surrounding the fate of the nation's undocumented immigrant population, the student voices presented here truly provide a unique perspective. The stories in this collection are moving and inspirational sagas of students emerging from the shadows, coping with issues of educational access, and demanding the promise of opportunity for all."

– Michael Omi, Associate Professor of Ethnic Studies, University of California, Berkeley

"Amid the shrill hue and cry over undocumented immigration, so often lacking in basic facts, Underground Undergrads *is an eye-opening, myth-busting, luminous gem of a book, humanizing and bringing to life the extraordinary stories of undocumented students who have made it to college against all odds. They*

came at an early age from El Salvador and Vietnam and Mexico and Korea and elsewhere, and have grown up American, speaking English, working hard, and demonstrating uncommon talents and values that can only redound to the lasting benefit of this society. Yet these students are denied basic rights and must live with daily indignities, blocked aspirations, and in constant fear of deportation. Well educated and refusing to be pushed further underground, they have emerged as committed activists for immigrant rights, inspired by and evoking the best of American traditions. These ambitious students are at once exemplars of the possibilities and contradictions of the United States, of the American dream in Deportation Nation."

– Rubén G. Rumbaut, Professor of Sociology, University of California, Irvine

"The young Bruins featured in this book represent some of the finest leaders of their generation. As someone who knows what it means to beat the odds and graduate with a UCLA diploma, I salute their drive and hard work in continuing the quest for the American dream. They are living proof that promoting immigrant integration is in the best interest of our city and of our nation."

– Antonio Villaraigosa, Mayor, City of Los Angeles

contents

Forward
Gilbert Cedillo ....*vi*

Instructors' Preface
Kent Wong, Janna Shadduck-Hernández,
and Gaspar Rivera-Salgado ....*ix*

Preface
Angelo A. Mathay ....*xii*

Acknowledgments ....*xiv*

Part I. Legislation
Armin M. Najafi

Legislation Timeline...2

Assembly Bill 540...5

The California Dream Act 10

The Federal Dream Act..13

Part II. Speaking Out

Amazing Grace 19
Mariana D. Zamboni

Fighting Another War 24
Erika Perez

A Downward Spiral 29
John Carlo

Pedagogy of a Student Activist 36
Fabiola Inzunza

Walking across the Stage.....................................41
Veronica Valdez

A Legacy of Colonization 47
Gregory Allan Cendana

Out of My Hands 52
Antonio Alvarez

Testimony of Tam Tran...57
Tam Tran

Vietnamese Refugee Family in Limbo..................60
Teresa Watanabe, Los Angeles Times

Immigrant's Family Detained after Daughter Speaks Out 62
Kathy Kiely, USA Today

Part III. Taking Action

Taking Action 66
Gabriela Madera and Wendell Pascual

Improving Dreams, Equality, Access, and Success (IDEAS) ..73
Wendy Escobar, Heidy A. Lozano,
and Fabiola Inzunza

Epilogue...76
Angelo A. Mathay

Resource Guide 79
Hector Saldivar

forward

Gilbert Cedillo

Senator Gilbert Cedillo. *Courtesy of Senator Cedillo's office.*

The historical context for this book is long and complex. California's intimate relationship with immigrants began centuries ago, and we can trace many of our best achievements to the overlapping contributions of multiple cultures. Early Mexican settlers in California established the basis for our modern system of medical care and were instrumental in drafting our constitution. During the 1900s, major expansions of industry in gold mining, railroads, and agriculture were achieved with Asian immigrant labor that included Chinese, Japanese, Filipino, and Korean migrants. The Transcontinental Railroad, the agricultural stronghold in central California, and the foundation for the farm workers' movement can all be traced to an immigrant's hand.

But these achievements are not without contradictions. The immigrant experience reflects the high and low points of our history. Whether celebrated, exploited, embraced, or shunned, immigrants—as settlers or as subjugates—were united by one theme: the pursuit of a more prosperous and hopeful future. This remains true today as an estimated 14 million undocumented immigrants, 2.5 million here in California, navigate a confusing landscape of contradictory laws and opportunities. Although undocumented immigrants constitute the fastest growing market segment for home mortgages, auto loans, credit cards, and insurance services, they cannot apply for drivers' licenses in many states, they face discriminatory, unconstitutional local laws, and they are continually denied due process and equal protection.

Contemporary migration patterns reflect the integration of our financial markets and trade. Unfortunately immigration and labor policies have not kept pace with this trend. Legal immigration channels are too restrictive relative to demand, resulting in an unnecessary increase in undocumented immigration. While we have made accommodations for the free flow of capital and the free trade of goods and services, we have simultaneously restricted the flow of labor that is a natural component of these transactions. Indeed we are restricting our greatest competitive asset—a mobile and increasingly affluent immigrant workforce—and limiting what can be leveraged to maintain our competitive position in the global economy.

California Sets the Tone

Because California has the largest population of undocumented immigrants in the nation, its future is inextricably linked with the future of the undocumented. With fully 90 percent of agricultural industries,

30 to 40 percent of service industries, and 20 percent of construction industries relying on an undocumented workforce, we can ill afford to ignore the issue.

In a recent report, the Public Policy Institute of California notes that at current graduation rates, the state is not capable of producing enough college graduates to meet future economic demand. The report suggests that the migration of college-educated workers from other states and countries will not fill our need. The authors advise the state to play an active role in enabling more Californians to obtain degrees, and they urge actions to increase educational attainment.

California has taken some action toward increasing access to higher education for all Californians. AB 540—the legislation granting in-state tuition to qualifying undocumented and documented students, which was first introduced by Senator Richard Polanco in 1992 and ultimately signed into law in 2001 under the stewardship of the late Assemblymember Marco Firebaugh—is a remarkable first step toward closing the opportunity gap. College remains financially untenable for most undocumented students, however, even those who work hard to earn top grades. Without a path to citizenship, a stable future remains out of reach for these remarkable young achievers.

To that end, I have introduced the California Dream Act in the state legislature. The bill proposes enabling qualified AB 540 students to apply for state financial aid, including institutional scholarships and some Cal Grant awards. At the federal level, the American Dream Act has been introduced in the House by two of California's representatives, Congressman Howard Berman and Congresswoman Lucille Roybal-Allard. This legislation would permit qualifying immigrant students to apply for citizenship after certain criteria have been met. It would also formalize provisions for in-state tuition for undocumented students at the federal level. Reform at both levels is necessary, as each bill resolves issues of concern within its jurisdiction. Without federal reform, a path to citizenship remains out of reach; without state reform, critical access to state financial aid may not be granted.

Distributing financial aid to our best and brightest students is not just a matter of immigration policy; it is an investment to secure our economic prosperity and a reflection of our mutually beneficial relationship with immigrants. Passage of the state and federal Dream Acts does not place one student's future above another's. It opens the door to higher education for all students.

Our Collective Stories and Shared Future

The story of reform is the collective story of millions of individuals in millions of households across the nation. The narrative is concerned with how immigration reform will play out at state and federal levels, whether we will be able to mobilize and educate the next generation of American immigrants, and how reform will affect the men, women, and children who have come to this country with the determination to create a better life.

Underground Undergrads encapsulates the personal stories of these individuals. This is a student publication, the culmination of coursework for Immigrant Rights, Labor, and Higher Education, a class offered through the UCLA Labor Center. Over the 2006–07 academic year, the students, with the help of their advisors, mapped out a body of research and fieldwork that became the basis for the book. They wrote and edited the content, helped develop the design, and oversaw publication. *Underground Undergrads* is the result of their work. It presents their stories.

The purpose of the book is twofold: to provide the historical context for immigration legislation in our nation, and to construct a framework for better understanding the various reform proposals at federal and state levels. Students also hope that the personal stories contained in this book will help shift some of the stereotypes and hateful rhetoric that have become so prevalent in the dialogue on immigration.

The stories and research data contained in this book are compelling. I commend the students' efforts in assembling such a timely and effective tool, and I urge you to use the book in your own efforts to effect change.

instructors' preface

Kent Wong, Janna Shadduck-Hernández, and Gaspar Rivera-Salgado

Kent Wong speaking at a press conference announcing the release of the "Unfulfilled Dreams" conference report.

Kent Wong is director of the UCLA Center for Labor Research and Education. Janna Shadduck-Hernández is a project director at the UCLA Downtown Labor Center. Both teach the course, Immigrant Rights, Labor, and Higher Education. Gaspar Rivera-Salgado is a project director at the UCLA Center for Labor Research and Education and teaches the summer internship program, Institute on Labor and the Workplace in Los Angeles.

May Day 2006 marked the largest immigrant rights demonstrations in U.S. history. In Los Angeles alone, two separate marches drew over one million people to the streets of the city. The immigrant rights struggle has emerged as the most significant civil rights movement of this generation.

The immigrant rights debate has a profound impact on millions of undocumented people living throughout the country. But there is one group of undocumented immigrants who face a particularly daunting challenge, and that is youth and students. The majority of these young people came to the United States as children, brought from their native lands by their parents or relatives.

UCLA, like every other public college and university in California, has a sizable undocumented student population.

Undocumented students at UCLA have beaten all odds to gain admission to one of the most prestigious public universities in the country. Yet they are ineligible for most financial aid and scholarships, they are prohibited from getting drivers' licenses, they are barred from taking out students loans, they cannot obtain work-study funds or work on campus, and upon graduation, they are not eligible to seek legal employment. Yet in spite of all these obstacles, they are among the most brilliant, dedicated, and compassionate students within the University of California.

The UCLA Center for Labor Research and Education has been involved with immigrant workers for many years, in large part because of the vast immigrant working class of Los Angeles. Many of the most successful organizing campaigns in Los Angeles have been led by immigrant workers, including janitors, hotel workers, laundry workers, construction workers, truck drivers, and home care and health care workers. We have conducted research on immigrant workers, hosted educational conferences on immigration, and sponsored the first Spanish-language

Janna Shadduck-Hernández and the class speak on KPFK radio about the Dream Act. *Photograph by Jessica Chou.*

leadership school in the country. The UCLA Downtown Labor Center, located near MacArthur Park, is establishing a resource center to address the needs of immigrant workers.

Through our UCLA minor in labor and workplace studies, we have encouraged students to intern with labor and community organizations that reach out to immigrant workers. In recent years, increasing numbers of undocumented immigrant students have taken our courses at UCLA. We were deeply moved by their stories and their painstaking efforts to complete their education in the face of overwhelming obstacles. Through these students, the Labor Center reached out to IDEAS, the student organization for UCLA undocumented students. We were amazed that in spite of their own personal hardships, they were volunteering precious time to support other undocumented students and to reach out to high school students to encourage them to attend college.

These students inspired us to take action. In Winter 2007, the UCLA Labor Center offered the very first class on undocumented students, Immigrant Rights, Labor, and Higher Education. This book is a product of that class. Our students, both documented and undocumented,

impressed us with their hard work and diligence. Regardless of their status, the students embraced this project as their own. They researched legal and legislative issues, conducted interviews, identified community resources, and collected photos, poems, and spoken-word pieces for the publication.

Our students also organized a hearing in May 2007 convened by five members of the California state legislature and attended by hundreds of community members. The hearing received substantial media coverage, and a hearing report produced by the students was distributed throughout the country. In Summer 2007, many of our students participated in an internship program through the UCLA Labor Center. They organized a hunger strike, press conferences, protest vigils, and dozens of speaking engagements and meetings. Some traveled to Sacramento to meet with leaders of the state legislature and the governor to talk about their experiences as undocumented students.

Unfortunately during the course of producing this book, undocumented students suffered two setbacks. In late 2007, the Federal DREAM Act failed to pass in Congress, in large part because of fierce opposition from Republicans. Shortly thereafter, the

Gaspar Rivera-Salgado speaking at a conference on AB 540 students organized by the UCLA Labor Center, May 19, 2007.

California Dream Act passed the state legislature but was vetoed by the governor. Our students' tremendous hopes to fulfill their educational and career aspirations were once again deferred. However, the campaign to realize their dreams continues.

The stories in this book reveal the hopes and aspirations of UCLA undocumented students, but they also represent millions of undocumented youth and students who are striving for the American dream. The UCLA Labor Center is honored to have had the opportunity of working with these extraordinary young people. We are fully confident that they will eventually win their fight for the full rights and privileges that they desperately need and deserve.

preface
Angelo A. Mathay

Generations after the civil rights movement, a new movement that follows a similar path is burgeoning in the United States. Students are at the head of this movement, which centers on immigrant rights, organizing, and mobilizing on a scale that the United States has not seen for decades. Because of its multicutural nature, Los Angeles is at the forefront of this movement. Student organizations in the Los Angeles area have banded together to influence the debate raging in Congress. What is surprising about this student-led movement is that a majority of these activists are undocumented. As undocumented residents, they face significant burdens and stigmas every day; yet they understand that the fight for their education is a necessity.

Although undocumented students are a major presence throughout the United States, the undocumented student movement is strongest in Southern California. With the passage of Assembly Bill 540 (authored by the late Marco Firebaugh) in 2001, these students have been given the opportunity to attend universities all over California. Nevertheless, most still have difficulty financing their education because they are unable to receive state or federal financial aid. They face the harsh reality of interrupting their educational careers to save money for tuition by working low-wage jobs despite the uncertainty of employment after receiving their college degrees. Many undergo tremendous emotional stress produced by the fear of deportation.

Undocumented students have been at the forefront of organizing for the passage of state and federal Dream Acts as well as lobbying for comprehensive immigration reform across the country. The issue of undocumented immigrants has become a transnational issue, with corporations and international institutions pushing for extensive immigration reform. Protecting undocumented immigrants from corporate exploitation has been difficult owing to the broken system of U.S. immigration laws but as the need for reform has become more apparent, more individuals are beginning to organize and take action.

The students who contributed to this publication are among those who are most committed to the immigrant rights movement. Many of these students participated in the Immigrant Rights, Labor, and Higher Education course at UCLA, taught by Kent Wong and Janna Shadduck-Hernández during the 2006–07 school year. During the first quarter of the class, students learned how to be ethnographers, and they transcribed accounts of their families' immigration histories. Through exercises, lectures, and discussions—and the remarks of inspiring guest speakers, such as Josh Bernstein from the National Immigration Law Center, Victor Narro from the UCLA Labor Center, and Michael Garcés from the Cornerstone Theater Company—students from the class were exposed to the many facets of the immigration debate.

For the second quarter of the course, the students separated into groups that focused on goals for this publication and a conference later in the quarter. The research and legislative group worked on outlining all the court cases and legislation that have played a role in the present state of U.S. immigration policy. The conference group worked on organizing a conference at UCLA that would present the stories of a select group of undocumented students and provide informational workshops on current legislation, strategies for organizing, and financing one's education while undocumented. The editing, layout, and design group worked on selecting and editing the family histories and interviews from the previous quarter for inclusion in this publication.

Each of the testimonials, interviews, and family histories that are collected in this volume was drawn from individuals who participated in the class and from other inspirational individuals class members worked with. These stories reflect the struggles of undocumented students throughout California and the nation. They focus on a wide array of experiences, from an eleven-year-old boy running away from home and joining revolutionaries in El Salvador, to a young woman testifying in front of the U.S. Congress and sharing her story as an undocumented student. These experiences gave class members a personal perspective on the contemporary immigration debate. They broadened their roles as student activists, participating in various immigrant rights events, such as May Day marches, radio shows, conferences, and symposiums.

Since the students completed the courses, some progress has been made in moving toward a resolution for undocumented students. As a result of persistent efforts from the students and their allies, a coalition of networks has been developed to place pressure on our representatives to support legislation that will help undocumented students pursue their educational goals. These bills include the California Dream Act at the state level and the DREAM Act at the federal level.

With Professor Kent Wong's and Professor Janna Shadduck-Hernández's encouragement, class members have promoted awareness about undocumented students in communities throughout the state of California. The immigration hearing and conference that was organized by this class and held at UCLA on May 19, 2007, was attended by key members of the California state legislature, including Senators Gilbert Cedillo and Gloria Romero, and Assemblymembers Anthony Portantino, Mike Eng, and Kevin De León. The ongoing debate in the U.S. Congress has galvanized many of these students to fight for immigrant rights and educate those who have been misinformed about the issue.

By educating and reaching out to citizens and political leaders who are unaware of the issue of undocumented college students, we believe that we will put comprehensive immigration reform and the Dream Act at the forefront of the discussion in Congress. As student activists, we are building on the tradition of the civil rights movement and promoting the passage of legislation that will enable millions of undocumented students to not only dream but also start living a life without borders.

acknowledgments

Spring 2007 Immigrant Rights, Labor, and Higher Education class. *Courtesy of UCLA Labor Center.*

The UCLA Labor Center would like to thank the dedicated students of the labor and workplace studies Winter and Spring 2007 course, Immigrant Rights, Labor, and Higher Education, who conducted interviews, researched legal issues, and wrote this book. Their work inspires us, and the stories that they tell move us. We are thankful to them for their amazing work. Members of the class were Mae Lapid Cauguiran, Gregory Allan Cendana, Wendy Carmen Escobar, Lourdes Galindo, Monique B. González, Jasmín Ibarra, Fabiola Inzunza, Heidy A. Lozano, Gabriela Madera, Angelo Arnaldo Mathay, Armin M. Najafi, Lisa Anne Nichols, Michael Beltran Ombao, Matías Arely Ortez, Nicolas Patino, Joanna Beatriz Perez, Ernesto Rocha, Héctor Hugo Saldívar, Alyssa Jane M. Titong, Victoria Valdés, Dina Afrahim, Saira Aisha Gandhi, Robert Allan Godzik, Gina Kim, Omar Rahman, Marla Andrea Ramirez, Phuong My Tran, David Paul Vallejo Jr., Yleana Velasco, and Mariana D. Zamboni.

Thank you to the UCLA Labor Center's 2007 summer interns, who saw to the completion of the book. Members of the publication team, Gabriela Madera, Angelo Arnaldo Mathay, Armin M. Najafi, Hector Hugo Saldívar, Alyssa Jane M. Titong, and Stephanie Solis, ardently focused on the production and release of the publication. Members of the education and outreach team, Gregory Cendana, Lourdes Galindo, Monique Gonzalez, Fabiola Inzunza, Susan Melgarejo, Nicolas Patino, Ernesto Rocha, Tam Tran, and Mariana D. Zamboni, committed themselves to immigration rights and educated our communities on the Dream Act.

The wonderful photographs, artwork, and poetry constitute one of the most important aspects of this publication. Those who contributed these pieces are talented students who made this publication even more vibrant. We extend our thanks to these contributors: Jessica Chou; Cora Cervantes; the members of IDEAS at UCLA as well as CHIRLA, for capturing images of the immigration movement; Mariana D. Zamboni, Maria Elizabeth, Yaocihuatl, Laura Marcela, Mario Escobar, and Antonio Guzman, for artistically expressing their life struggles through poetry; and John Carlo, Carol Montes, and Miriam Delgado, for their beautiful drawings and paintings.

We would like to thank the authors and students who contributed to the stories in this publication, and we are also grateful to Senator Gilbert Cedillo for authoring the forward. Special thanks go to the production team of Rebecca Frazier, Wendell Pascual, and Heather Henderson, and to the staff of the UCLA Labor Center: Joaquin Calderón, Elizbeth Espinoza, Cristina López, Julie Monroe, Victor Narro, Gaspar Rivera-Salgado, Janna Shadduck-Hernández, and Kent Wong.

Lastly we thank all groups, organizations, leaders, and communities who have supported the production of the publication, including Josh Bernstein, Melinna Bobadilla, Meredith Brown, Senator Gilbert Cedillo, Xiomara Corpeño, Hugo Cristales, Assemblymember Kevin De León, Fernando de Necochea, María Elena Durazo, Assemblymember Mike Eng, Alfred Herrera, Russell Jauregui, Erik Lee, Speaker of the Assembly Fabian Núñez, Keith Parker, Marvin Pineda, Assemblymember Anthony Portantino, Maria Rodriguez, Senator Gloria Romero, Angélica Salas, and Henry Walton. We deeply appreciate your continued commitment to the struggle for immigrant rights.

Part I

LEGISLATION

Armin M. Najafi

Students hold a candlelight vigil in Sacramento for the Dream Act, August 19, 2007. *Photograph by Susan Melgarejo.*

Legislation Timeline

1980:
The Uniform Residency Law
(California law)

From 1974 until 1980, the Uniform Residency Law of California provided an exemption that allowed long-term California residents to pay in-state tuition at all California public colleges and universities. The law sunsetted in 1980 without being renewed. From 1980 until 1986, undocumented students were charged out-of-state tuition at all California public colleges and universities.[1]

1982:
Plyler v. Doe

In 1982 the United States Supreme Court overturned a Texas law that barred the children of undocumented immigrants from public elementary and secondary schools (K-12). The court's ruling affirmed that elementary and secondary education is a fundamental right for all children, regardless of their immigration and legal status.[2]

1985:
Leticia A. v. UC Regents and CSU Board of Trustees

In 1985 the Alameda County Superior Court ruled that undocumented students should be treated as California residents for the purposes of paying in-state tuition. Students who met the residency requirements of one year and one day qualified to pay in-state tuition and were eligible for state financial aid in the form of Cal Grants.[3] (A Cal Grant is money provided by the State of California to students who attend colleges in California and are qualified to receive aid. Cal Grants do not have to be paid back.)[4]

1986:
Immigration Reform and Control Act (IRCA)
(federal law)

Passed in 1986, IRCA was the last comprehensive federal immigration law passed in the United States. IRCA's main provisions included: 1) amnesty for undocumented immigrants who could prove residency for a number of years; 2) imposed criminal and civil penalties against employers who knowingly hired undocumented immigrants;[5] and 3) disbursement of approximately $4 billion to state and local

Artistic Drawing: IDEAS
My name is Carol Belisa Montes. I was born in San Pedro Sula, Honduras. My parents immigrated to the United States in 1988 along with my younger sister and me. The only friends I found loyal were my sketchbook and my mediums (paint, pencil, pen, or charcoal). I am an artist, and art helps me express myself in many ways. Even my artist name, Mocabel, is art in itself, and it means Montes Carol Belisa. I was born in the lands of the America, I was raised and educated in America, but I am not American. I am what the United States calls an alien. But I am an alien that has been fighting and will continue to fight until I get my rights as a U.S citizen, because this is the "Land of Opportunities."

governments for welfare and education programs. Approximately 3 million people had their immigration status legalized under IRCA.[6]

1990:
Bradford v. UC Regents

The *Leticia A.* ruling was effectively overturned in Los Angeles County Superior Court in 1990. Following the court's decision, undocumented students were charged out-of-state tuition and lost all eligibility to receive state or federal financial aid.[7]

1994:
Proposition 187
(California ballot initiative)

Proposition 187, passed by California voters in 1994, called for the denial of access to public education, child welfare, and non-emergency health care (e.g., immunizations) for all undocumented immigrants.[8] Prop 187 was ultimately overturned by the United States Supreme Court in 1995. The court declared that by denying privileges to undocumented immigrants, the State was unconstitutionally regulating immigration, which only the federal government can legislate.[9]

1996:
Illegal Immigration Reform and Immigrant Responsibility Act (IIRIRA)
(federal law)

Section 505 of IIRIRA prohibits states from offering higher education benefits to undocumented students without offering those same benefits to U.S. citizens and nationals who meet certain criteria. AB 540 and similar legislation was drafted in such a way so that all students who meet specific requirements are eligible for its benefits.[10]

Benefits Derived from Higher Education

1. An individual with an associate's degree earns, on average, $207,600 more over his or her lifetime than a person with a high school diploma. A bachelor's degree yields $590,000 and a professional degree $1,839,100 more than a high school diploma.[11]

2. The median annual income in 2001 was $35,000 for those with high school degrees, $56,000 for those with bachelor's degrees, $71,000 for those with master's degrees, and $100,000 for those with professional degrees.[12]

3. A college degree also has noneconomic benefits. For example, college graduates are healthier, commit fewer crimes, and participate more fully in community life.[13]

Numbers and Figures

1. California has over 25,000 undocumented students graduating from California high schools each year.[14]

2. Each year 50,000 to 65,000 undocumented students graduate from U.S. high schools.[15]

3. In 2005–06, 1,483 University of California students received AB 540 nonresident fee exemptions. Of those, 1,061 were documented students, and 32 were students who were petitioning for visas, leaving a total of 390 students who were potentially undocumented.[16]

4. Many undocumented students don't take advantage of state policies that would allow them to pay in-state tuition because they are not aware of them or view college as financially inaccessible because they are not eligible for financial aid.[17]

1. Committee on Education, Bill Analysis of AB 1197, July 7, 1999, 4. Available at the California State Senate web site, http://info.sen.ca.gov/pub/99-00/bill/asm/ab_1151-1200/ab_1197_cfa_19990706_164545_sen_comm.html.
2. Paz M. Oliverez et al, eds., "The College and Financial Aid Guide for: AB540 Undocumented Immigrant Students," Center for Higher Education Policy Analysis, University of Southern California, October 2006, 16. Available at http://www.fao.ucla.edu/Forms/pdfs/07_08_ab540students.pdf.
3. Ibid, 17.
4. For a definition of a Cal Grant and more information, see the California Student Aid Commission web site, http://www.calgrants.org.
5. Leo R. Chavez, *Shadowed Lives: Undocumented Immigrants in American Society* (Fort Worth: Harcourt Brace, 1998), 20.
6. Ibid, 12.
7. Liz Guillen, "Undocumented Immigrant Students: A Very Brief Overview of Access to Higher Education in California," 1. Available at Teaching to Change LA web site, http://tcla.gseis.ucla.edu/reportcard/features/5-6/ab540/pdf/UndocImmigStud.pdf. See also "Immigration Law—Education—California Extends Instate Tuition Benefits to Undocumented Aliens," *Harvard Law Review* 115, no. 5 (2002): 1550.
8. Caroline J. Tolbert and Rodney E. Hero, "Race/Ethnicity and Direct Democracy: An Analysis of California's Illegal Immigration Initiative," *The Journal of Politics* 58, no. 3 (1996): 806.
9. Monica Guizar, "Facts About Federal Preemption: How to analyze whether state and local initiatives are an unlawful attempt to enforce federal immigration law or regulate immigration," June 2007, 3. Available at the National Immigration Law Center web site, http://www.nilc.org/immlawpolicy/LocalLaw/federalpreemptionfacts_2007-06-28.pdf.
10. Paz M. Oliverez.
11. "Immigration Law—Education—California Extends Instate Tuition Benefits to Undocumented Aliens."
12. Paz M. Oliverez.
13. "Immigration Law—Education—California Extends Instate Tuition Benefits to Undocumented Aliens," 1548.
14. "California Dream Act—SB160 (Cedillo) Fact Sheet." Available at the Orange County Dream Team web site, http://www.istillhaveadream.org/Dream_20Act-_20Fact_20sheet.pdf.
15. Paz M. Oliverez.
16. "Senate Appropriations Committee Fiscal Summary," Senator Tom Torlakson, Chairman, Bill Analysis of SB160. Available at the California State Senate web site, http://info.sen.ca.gov/pub/07-08/bill/sen/sb_0151-0200/sb_160_cfa_20070531_180340_sen_comm.html.
17. Karen Fisher, "Illegal Immigrants Rarely Use Hard-Won Tuition Break," *The Chronicle of Higher Education* 51, no. 16 (2004): A19.

Assembly Bill 540

AB 540 History

Assembly Bill 540 (AB 540), authored by the late Marco A. Firebaugh, makes higher education more accessible for undocumented students. The bill was passed by the California State Senate and State Assembly in September 2001.[1] AB 540 became law when Governor Gray Davis signed the bill on October 11, 2001.[2] In January 2002, the law took effect in the California Community College and California State University systems. Soon after, the University of California Board of Regents voted to adopt AB 540.[3]

Former Assemblymember Marco Antonio Firebaugh. *Courtesy of former Assemblymember Firebaugh's office.*

What Is AB 540?

AB 540 is a California law that allows out-of-state students and undocumented students who meet certain requirements to be exempt from paying nonresident tuition at all public colleges and universities in California.[4]

What Are the Requirements?

In order for a student to be eligible for AB 540, he or she must fulfill the following requirements:

1. The student must have attended a California high school for three or more years.
2. The student must have graduated from a California high school or attained an equivalent degree (e.g., a General Education Diploma, or GED).
3. The student must be currently enrolled or registered as an entering student at an accredited institution of higher education in California.[5]

Affidavit Process for Undocumented Students Only

Once all these requirements have been fulfilled, an undocumented student must fill out an affidavit with the institute of higher education that states that he or she has filed an application to regularize his or her immigration status, or will file an application as soon as he or she is eligible to do so.[6]

All Information Given by a Student Remains Confidential

Undocumented students do not need to worry that any information they give pertaining to their immigration status will be used against them in any way. Any information given by a student is protected under the Family Education Rights and Privacy Act (FERPA). A federal law passed in 1974, FERPA protects the privacy of a student's education records.[7] In other words, the U.S. Immigration and Customs Enforcement (ICE) cannot access a student's education records.

Why Is AB 540 Necessary?

The California state legislature made its decision to adopt AB 540 and exempt undocumented students from paying nonresident tuition for three main reasons:

1. The legislature found that many undocumented high school students had attended elementary and secondary schools in the state of California and were likely to remain in the state but were precluded from obtaining an affordable college education because they were required to pay nonresident tuition (see table 1).
2. The legislature agreed that it was unjust to deny these students higher education, since they had already proven their academic eligibility and merit by being accepted into California's colleges and universities.

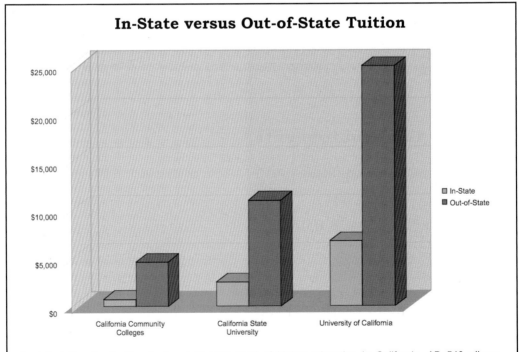

In-State versus Out-of-State Tuition

In-state tuition is significantly lower at each level of higher education in California. AB 540 allows undocumented students to pay in-state fees of approximately $780 a year, versus $4,620 for out-of-state fees, at California Community Colleges; $2,552 versus $11,010 at California State University campuses; and $6,780 versus $24,900 at University of California campuses.

3. Finally they concluded that a fair tuition policy for all high school pupils in California ensures access to California's colleges and universities and thereby increases the state's collective productivity and economic growth.[8]

How Do Students Apply for AB 540?

Once a student is accepted into a California college or university, he or she should immediately apply for AB 540 status. A student can begin the process either by picking up a California Nonresident Tuition Exemption Request or the University of California Nonresident Tuition Exemption Application and Affidavit at the registrar's office on campus or by downloading the appropriate form from the school's web site.

Limitations of AB 540

1. AB 540 does not give undocumented students access to state or federal financial aid.
2. AB 540 does not provide a venue to undocumented students for adjusting their immigration status.

Other States with Similar Legislation[9]

Several states have passed laws or are considering laws that are similar to AB 540.[10]

1. *Texas.* In 2001 Texas became the first state to allow undocumented students to pay in-state tuition. Texas is also the only state in which undocumented students are eligible to receive state financial aid.
2. *Utah and New York.* In 2002 both states enacted legislation that allows undocumented students to pay in-state tuition.
3. *Washington, Oklahoma, and Illinois.* In 2003 and 2004 these three states passed legislation that allows undocumented students to pay in-state tuition.
4. *Kansas.* In 2004 Kansas passed legislation that allowed undocumented students to pay in-state tuition.[11]
5. *New Mexico.* New Mexico does not have a state law that allows undocumented students to pay in-state tuition, but some institutions have been granting in-state tuition as well as providing some tuition exemptions for undocumented students.
6. *Nebraska.* Nebraska became the tenth state to pass legislation that provides a path for undocumented students to pay in-state tuition for higher education.
7. *Other States.* Similar legislation is pending in Colorado, Connecticut, Florida, Hawaii, Massachusetts, Minnesota, New Hampshire, New Jersey, North Carolina, South Carolina, Oregon, Tennessee, and Virginia.[12]

1. "Immigration Law—Education—California Extends Instate Tuition Benefits to Undocumented Aliens," *Harvard Law Review* 115, no. 5 (2002): 1548–54.
2. Ibid, 1550.
3. AB 540 required the Trustees of the California State University and the Board of Governors of the California Community Colleges, and requested the Regents of the University of California, to adopt AB 540. In other words, it was up to the discretion of the UC Regents whether to adopt AB 540.
4. "Assembly Bill No. 540, Chapter 814," 3. Available at the Immigrant Legal Resource Center web site, http://www.ilrc.org/ab540bill.pdf.
5. "Assembly Bill Number: 540," Chapter 814. Available at the Mexican American Legal Defense and Educational Fund web site, http://www.maldef.org/ab540/pdf/AB_540.pdf.
6. Ibid.
7. Paz M. Oliverez et al, eds., "The College and Financial Aid Guide for: AB540 Undocumented Immigrant Students," Center for Higher Education Policy Analysis, University of Southern California, October 2006, 16. Available at http://www.fao.ucla.edu/Forms/pdfs/07_08_ab540students.pdf.
8. California Assembly Committee on Higher Education.
9. Radha Roy Biswas, "Access to Community College for Undocumented Immigrants: A Guide for State Policymakers," Achieving the Dream policy brief, 2005. Available at Indiana Pathways to College Network web site, http://inpathways.net/AccessCommunityColleges.pdf.
10. The states with the largest undocumented immigrant populations are: California (2.2 million), Texas (1.0 million), New York (0.5 million), Illinois (0.4 million), and Florida (0.3 million). Migration Policy Institute, "Unauthorized Immigration to the United States," October 2003. Available at http://www.migrationpolicy.org/pubs/USImmigrationFacts2003.pdf.
11. National Conference of State Legislatures, "In-state Tuition and Unauthorized Immigrant Students," April, 26, 2006. Available at http://www.ncsl.org/programs/immig/tuitionandimmigrants.htm.
12. Josh Bernstein, "Court Upholds California In-state Tuition Law (AB 540)," October 10, 2006. Available at the National Immigration Law Center web site, http://www.nilc.org/immlawpolicy/DREAM/Dream006.htm.

Increased **financial aid**
for all students
in California's
universities and colleges

Rally for the Dream Act. *Courtesy of Jessica Chou.*

increases the state's
collective productivity and
economic growth.

The California Dream Act

History of the California Dream Act

The California Dream Act is proposed legislation authored and introduced by California State Senator Gilbert Cedillo. The first version of the California Dream Act (SB 160) was heard and passed by the Senate Education Committee on April 28, 2005.[1] Despite popular support, SB 160 was vetoed by Governor Arnold Schwarzenegger in September 2006.[2] In 2007 Senator Cedillo reintroduced an identical bill also named the California Dream Act (SB 65). The state legislature never had the opportunity to vote on SB 65 since the bill failed to pass the Assembly Rules Committee.[3] The third version of the California Dream Act (SB 1) differed from earlier versions of the bill in the sense that many provisions found in SB 160 and SB 65 were amended to address the governor's veto message.[4] SB 1 was passed by the state legislature on September 12, 2007.[5] Despite the changes made to SB 1, Governor Schwarzenegger vetoed this version of the California Dream Act on October 13, 2007.[6]

What Is the California Dream Act?

The California Dream Act would allow undocumented AB 540 students to apply for state and institutional financial aid without the use of the Federal Application for Student Aid (FAFSA).[7] Current law does not allow undocumented students to qualify for any financial aid regardless of their economic need. The three different versions of the California Dream Act would allow undocumented students to apply for various types of aid.

Types of Financial Aid Available

SB 160 and SB 65 would have allowed students to apply for three types of aid:

1. Board of Governors (BOG) Fee Waivers. Current law authorizes the Board of Governors of the California Community Colleges (CCC) to waive college fees for low-income students. The California Dream Act would require community college districts to waive the fees of undocumented AB 540 students who qualify for a waiver under the standards established by the Board of Governors.[8]
2. Institutional Student Aid. Institutional aid is any financial aid program

administered by a college or university. This bill would allow undocumented students to apply for institutional aid, including State University Grants at the California State University (CSU) and the UC Grant at the University of California (UC).

3. State-Administered Student Aid. Undocumented students would be eligible to receive state-funded financial aid programs including, but not limited to, Cal Grants.[9]

Amending the Provisions of Qualifying for AB 540 Status

The California Dream Act (SB 160 and SB 65) would also amend some of the requirements to qualify for AB 540 status under the California Education Code (§ 68130.5).[10] Under this bill, to be eligible for AB 540 status, a student would be required to attend (for at least three years) and graduate from a California secondary school, but students graduating from technical schools and adult schools would be eligible for AB 540 status, in addition to students graduating from traditional high schools.

The Difference between SB 1 and Earlier Versions of the California Dream Act

SB 1 differed from earlier versions of the California Dream Act in that it did not give undocumented students access to competitive financial aid.[11] AB 540 students would be eligible to apply for any financial aid program administered by the State of California, except the Competitive Cal Grant A and B award program.[12] Unlike previous versions of the bill, SB 1 would not have given undocumented students access to institutional aid, nor would it have amended the provisions for qualifying for AB 540 status.

The California Dream Act proposals do not grant undocumented students any advantage over the student population as a whole in determining who qualifies for, or receives, financial aid.[13] The California Dream Act would give undocumented students the opportunity to apply for financial aid; whether they receive aid is determined by the same standards that are used in evaluating other students who apply for financial aid.

Why Is the California Dream Act Necessary?

Every year 50,000 to 65,000 undocumented students graduate from U.S. high schools.[14] Senator Orrin Hatch, author of earlier versions of the federal Dream Act, noted that "many of these youngsters find themselves caught in a catch-22 situation. As [undocumented] immigrants, they cannot work legally. They are also effectively barred from developing academically beyond high school because of the high cost of pursuing higher education. In short, although these children have built their lives here, they have no possibility of achieving and living the American dream. What a tremendous loss for them, and what a tremendous loss to our society."[15]

AB 540 did alleviate some of the financial burdens faced by undocumented students in California by making them eligible for in-state, as opposed to out-of-state, tuition. Despite the success of AB 540, in-state tuition remains outside the economic reach of many undocumented students. The California Dream Act would help not only undocumented students but also the state. The California State Senate attested to this fact by declaring that "increased financial aid for all students in California's universities and colleges increases the state's collective productivity and economic growth."[16] Senator Cedillo emphasizes how this bill would benefit the state of California: "We have made an investment of 12 years of public education in these children already. It makes no sense to undermine that investment by not granting them funding available to every high-school student."[17]

Support for the California Dream Act

As of April 2006, the California State University Board of Trustees, the University of California Regents, and the California Community College Board of Governors all openly supported this bill. Despite the overwhelming support for the California Dream Act by all the major institutions for higher education in California, Governor Schwarzenegger continues to oppose this bill.

1. "Senate Committee on Education," John Scott, Chair, Bill Analysis of SB 160. Available at the California State Senate web site, http://info.sen.ca.gov/pub/07-08/bill/sen/sb_0151-0200/sb_160_cfa_20070313 _094916_sen_comm.html.
2. Paz M. Oliverez et al, eds., "The College and Financial Aid Guide for: AB540 Undocumented Immigrant Students," Center for Higher Education Policy Analysis, University of Southern California, October 2006, 18. Available at http://www.fao.ucla.edu/Forms/pdfs/07_08_ab540students.pdf.
3. California Postsecondary Education Commission, "Legislative Update," August 2007. Available at http://www.cpec.ca.gov/Agendas/Agenda0708/Item_01.pdf.
4. "California Dream Act, SB 160 (Cedillo)." Available at Senator Gilbert Cedillo web site, http://dist22.casen .govoffice.com/index.asp?Type=B_PR&SEC={618F8B21-E3F2-436F-AD33-4F47062FA1BD}.
5. "Senate Bill No. 1." Available at the California State Senate web site, http://info.sen.ca.gov/pub/07-08/bill/ sen/sb_0001-0050/sb_1_bill_20070917_enrolled.pdf.
6. Patrick McGreevy, "Bills Opposed by NRA Signed: Legislation Making it Easier for Police to Trace Bullets and Banning Lead Ammo in Condor Habitat Becomes Law," *Los Angeles Times*, October 14, 2007. Available at http://www.latimes.com.
7. "California Dream Act—SB160 (Cedillo) Fact Sheet." Available at the Orange County Dream Team web site, http://www.istillhaveadream.org/Dream_20Act-_20Fact_20sheet.pdf.
8. "Senate Bill No. 65." Available at the California State Senate web site, http://info.sen.ca.gov/pub/07-08/bill/ sen/sb_0051-0100/sb_65_bill_20070625_amended_asm_v95.pdf.
9. Ibid.
10. Ibid.
11. Telephone interview with Eric Guerra, legislative aide to Senator Gilbert Cedillo, September 21, 2007.
12. Cal Grants A and B are distributed based on a student's grade point average. Previous versions of the California Dream Act (SB 160 and SB 65) made these grants available to undocumented students. The latest version (SB 1) gives undocumented students access to Cal Grant C, which is based solely on a student's financial need. For more information on Cal Grants, see the California Student Aid Commission web site, http://www.calgrants.org.
13. "Senate Bill No. 160." Available at the California State Senate web site, http://info.sen.ca.gov/pub/07-08/ bill/sen/sb_0151-0200/sb_160_bill_20070502_amended_sen_v98.pdf.
14. Paz M. Oliverez.
15. "California Dream Act—SB 160 (Cedillo) Fact Sheet."
16. "Senate Bill No. 160."
17. "College for All: San Francisco Chronicle Editorial of Support for the California Dream Act," *San Francisco Chronicle*, June 1, 2007.

The Federal Dream Act

History of the Dream Act

*The Dream Act was first introduced in 2001 during the 107th Congress.[1] The orig-
inal Dream Act failed to garner enough support to come to the floor for a vote.
Despite its initial failure, various forms of the Dream Act have been reintroduced
in the Senate and the House of Representatives, either as separate bills or as part
of larger, comprehensive immigration bills (see Table 2). The Senate version is
called the Development, Relief, and Education for Alien Minors Act, more commonly
referred to as the DREAM Act. The House version is formally called the American
Dream Act. Since their introduction in 2001, these versions of the Dream Act have
had forty-eight cosponsors in the Senate and more than one hundred fifty-two
cosponsors in the House.[2] Despite their popularity and bipartisan support, the bills
have been prevented from coming to the floor for a vote in either house by a minority that opposes the bills.[3] The most recent attempt to pass the Dream Act failed in
October 2007.*

Bills with Dream Act Provisions in the 110th Congress*

Senate	House
S 774 Development, Relief, and Education for Alien Minors (DREAM) Act	HR 1221 Education Access for Rightful Noncitizens (EARN) Act
S 1639 Unaccompanied Alien Child Protection Act	HR 1275 American Dream Act
S 1348 Comprehensive Immigration Reform Act	HR 1645 Security Through Regularized Immigration and a Vibrant Economy (STRIVE) Act

*Proposals will include language that would:
1. Amend the IIRIRA to permit states to determine state residency for higher education purposes.
2. Authorize the cancellation or removal and adjustment of status of certain unauthorized students who are long-term U.S. residents and entered the United States as children.

Dawn Konet, "Unauthorized Youths and Higher Education: The Ongoing Debate," September 2007. Available at the Migration Policy Insitute web site, http://www.migrationinformation.org/feature/display.cfm?ID=642.

An **undocumented student** who has studied for eight years to receive an MD **cannot** legally **practice** medicine . . . an undocumented student with a PhD cannot **teach** at a U.S. university.

Drawing of the federal Dream Act. *By Lizbeth.*
The reason I did that drawing is because somehow I'm kind of obsessed with trees. Trees are a source of life, and I believe we are like trees, or at least I think I'm like a tree. I have roots very deep into my Mexican culture, and I'm digging more into my indigenous culture as an Oaxaqueña. But the drawing represents all AB 540/undocumented students who have roots in other countries but who still hope and work hard toward achieving the American dream. If this country was a tree, we, the students, are the roots, the trunk. We are the whole tree. We are the source of life and the future of our communities, the future of this place, which is now our home, for some our only home; therefore, our roots are deep in this soil.

What Is the Federal Dream Act?

The Dream Act is legislation that will provide a path to legalization for certain undocumented students who were brought to the United States as children, completed their primary and secondary education in the United States, and fulfilled other requirements pertaining to education and contributing to the country.[4] The Dream Act will help these students by:

1. *Amending the Illegal Immigration Reform and Immigrant Responsibility Act (IIRIRA).* Section 505 of IIRIRA, which was enacted in 1996, prohibits states from giving undocumented students higher education benefits without making those same benefits available to U.S. citizens and legal permanent residents.[5] Repealing Section 505 of IIRIRA would permit states to determine the qualifications for state residency for the purposes of higher education benefits.
2. *Offering Conditional Permanent Resident Status.* Conditional permanent resident status is similar to lawful permanent resident status. The only difference is that it is valid for only six years. Undocumented students who have been given conditional permanent resident status would be able to work, drive, go to school, and participate in a number of other activities from which they are currently barred because of their undocumented status. They would also be eligible for federal work-study programs, student loans, and state-funded financial aid. They would not be eligible to receive Pell Grants or certain other federal financial aid grants, nor would they be permitted to travel abroad for lengthy periods of time.[6]

Who Can Qualify for Conditional Permanent Resident Status?

Under the Dream Act, undocumented students can have their immigration status adjusted to conditional permanent resident status if they meet the following criteria:

1. Students must have immigrated to the United States prior to reaching sixteen years of age and at least five years before the passage of the act.
2. Students must be of good moral character (e.g., a student convicted of a crime would not qualify).
3. At the time of submitting their applications, students must be admitted to an institution of higher education in the United States, must have graduated from high school, or must have received a General Education Diploma (GED) in the United States.

Qualifying for Lawful Permanent Resident Status

Regular lawful permanent resident status will be granted at the end of the conditional period of six years if immigrants have demonstrated good moral character and have completed at least one of the following criteria:

1. Students must graduate from a college or university in the United States or have completed at least two years of study toward a bachelor's or higher degree.
2. Students must have served in the armed forces for at least two years and, if discharged, have received an honorable discharge.

Previous versions of the Dream Act included a third option of completing 910 hours of community service.[7] That option has been omitted from the most recent drafts of the bill.

Why Is the Federal Dream Act Necessary?

Under current law, undocumented students who have earned degrees from the nation's top universities are unable to use those degrees or the skills they learned to find legal employment. For example, an undocumented student who has studied for eight years to receive an MD cannot legally practice medicine; an undocumented student who has earned a JD is not allowed to take the bar exam; an undocumented student with a PhD cannot teach at a U.S. university. Senator Dianne Feinstein stressed the necessity of the Dream Act stating that it "offers bright and highly motivated students a real incentive to become responsible and valued members of our society. Every year 50,000 undocumented children graduate from our nation's high schools or receive the equivalent of a secondary degree. From there they can take one of two paths: they can look at the hopelessness of their situation and get involved in crime, even join street gangs; or they can continue their education, find a good job, and give back something to the United States."[8]

Senate Majority Leader Harry Reid reiterated Senator Feinstein's sentiments after the most recent version of the federal Dream Act (S. 2205) failed to gain the sixty votes needed to pass the legislation: "What a waste it is to make it more difficult for children to go to college or get jobs, when they could be making meaningful contributions to their communities and to our country."[9]

1. National Immigration Law Center, "DREAM Act: Basic Information," October 2007. Available at http://www .nilc.org/immlawpolicy/DREAM/dream_basic_info_0406.pdf.
2. Ibid.
3. National Immigration Law Center, "DREAM Act Summary," April 2006, 1 Available at http://www.nilc .org/immlawpolicy/DREAM/dream_act_06_summary_2006-04.pdf.
4. Paz M. Oliverez et al, eds., "The College and Financial Aid Guide for: AB540 Undocumented Immigrant Students," Center for Higher Education Policy Analysis, University of Southern California, October 2006, 16. Available at http://www.fao.ucla.edu/Forms/pdfs/07_08_ab540students.pdf.
5. National Immigration Law Center, "DREAM Act: Basic Information." See also Paz M. Oliverez.
6. National Immigration Law Center, "DREAM Act Summary," 2.
7. National Immigration Law Center, "DREAM Act Reintroduced in Senate," *Immigrants' Rights Update*, 17, no. 5 (2003). Available at http://www.nilc.org/immlawpolicy/DREAM/Dream001.htm.
8. "Senator Feinstein Co-Sponsors 'The Dream Act.'" Available at U.S. Senator Dianne Feinstein web site, http://feinstein.senate.gov/03Releases/r-dreamact.htm. For more information on the positive benefits of the Dream Act, see National Immigration Law Center, "The Economic Benefits of the DREAM Act and the Student Adjustment Act," February 2005. Available at http://www.nilc.org/immlawpolicy/DREAM/Econ _Bens_DREAM&Stdnt_Adjst_0205.pdf.
9. Klaus Marre, "DREAM Act Fails to Clear Cloture Hurdle," *The Hill*, October 24, 2007.

Part II

SPEAKING OUT

The fast took its toll on participating students. *Photograph by Gabriel Madera.*

Amazing Grace. *Courtesy of Grace Lee.*

InVisible. *By Mariana Zamboni.*

Can you see her pain?
Can you taste her tears?
Would you want to know the injustices that she
hears?
Do you care?
Do you feel?
Would you want her to heal?
She feeds herself with hope
And drinks faith after every meal.
She lives in an illusionary world
Every time she kneels.
She's a slave in the land of the free
Sealed with 2 letters and 3 numbers;
Sealed with indifference and fear.

She's just a human, why do you wanna kill?
You are killing her inside
Every time you deny
Her existence in this land
Just cus she's not a US citizen
Doesn't mean she can't fly
But until you accept her
She continues to die.

amazing grace
Mariana D. Zamboni

Mariana interviewed Grace Lee for this profile of an academically promising Korean immigrant student who reached a crossroads and was forced to make a life-altering decision about her immigration status. Although this is a real account of an undocumented student's life, a pseudonym has been used to protect the identity of the person profiled.

Grace's kindness drew me to her one day while we were attending the same tutoring session offered by the Academic Advancement Program at UCLA. As our friendship developed, I learned that we share a secret: the secret of feeling invisible due to our immigration status. We both know what it means to be an undocumented immigrant student in one of the most prestigious universities in the United States. This is a glimpse into the life of my friend, an amazing young Korean American college woman.

Grace lived a comfortable life with her parents and two siblings in South Korea. Her mother was a housewife, and her father owned a construction business. Through the collective efforts of additional family members, Grace's family was well-off. She lived a happy and pleasant life until she was eleven years old, when suddenly things started to change.

I remember it was around 1997. Korea didn't have money, so we were going through IMF, where we had to borrow money from the USA. Most businesses were going out of business because [of] bankruptcy, and my dad's company was one of them.

The International Monetary Fund (IMF) helps oversee global financial systems and acts like a bank by offering countries financial and technical assistance. South Korea became one of these countries in need, and Grace's family was just one of many impacted by globalization. The economic instability in South Korea forced her family to seek various ways to survive. Migration became the solution.

Grace's father decided to immigrate to Canada in 1996 because "in Canada you don't need a visa. You can just go." It was the farthest he could travel from Korea without a visa. Despite his fervent desire to work and send money to his family in South Korea, he was unable to find a job for nine months. In addition to the economic uncertainty he was facing, Grace's father also faced the emotional burdens of being apart from his wife and children. Very few Koreans lived in Canada, and he felt very isolated. Because he was having difficulty adjusting, the rest of the Lee family moved to Canada to be reunited with him.

Living in Canada was difficult and as a result, Grace's parents thought about

The talk with her counselor gave Grace hope. **Dreams** that had faded because she lacked a **nine-digit** number were reawakened.

moving again. They believed that Los Angeles would offer them better economic, educational, and social opportunities. To achieve the dream of moving to Los Angeles, Grace, her mother, and her siblings returned to South Korea because they wanted to enter the United States legally. They purchased student visas and moved to Los Angeles.

Unfortunately Grace's father was not able to return to South Korea because he had fled the country illegally after filing for bankruptcy. Grace's father had no option but to enter the United States illegally. He paid a smuggler to drive him from Canada to Los Angeles, while he hid in the trunk of a car for three hours. I thought about how the media bombards us with images of undocumented Latino immigrants being smuggled across the Mexican border, but it is rare to hear of an undocumented Asian immigrant entering the United States in this manner.

Grace's parents believed that living in Koreatown, a district near downtown Los Angeles, would be detrimental for their acquisition of the English language. As a result, they settled in a city in the San Fernando Valley. Grace felt a sense of security and stability as she began her new life in the United States. Little did she know that it was just the beginning of a difficult journey.

Grace was eleven when she moved to Los Angeles in 1998. Regardless of the private tutoring in English that she had received

in South Korea, her knowledge of the language was rudimentary, and she was not able to communicate well. She remembers using an electronic dictionary often. Her English-as-a-second-language (ESL) teacher helped her gain confidence with her English verbal abilities. Grace also counted on her mother's encouragement to pursue higher education.

My mom always told me, "You have to go to college or else you'll end up like your dad and me . . . If you want to have better opportunities, and you want better for your children later on, you need to go to college and get a degree." So I always had that in the back of my mind.

The high school that Grace attended was in a lower-income neighborhood and had few Korean students, which her mother believed would encourage her children to practice English. Grace had high academic potential; she graduated with a 4.23 grade point average and was valedictorian of her class.

I was surprised to learn that Grace was not undocumented during high school. Because she had entered the country on a student visa, she was considered an international student. Although she was not classified as an undocumented immigrant on paper, she felt as if she were living the life of an undocumented immigrant student because of her inability to access benefits given to those with proof of U.S. citizenship—fee waivers, most scholarships, financial aid and many academic enrichment programs, and a driver's license. Although Grace had the opportunity to renew her student visa, she chose not to. She gave up her status as an international student visa holder in exchange for being an undocumented immigrant so that she could qualify for in-state tuition under AB 540. This decision was based on the knowledge Grace acquired from her older sister and college friends who were benefiting from the legislation.

Grace was aware that undocumented immigrant students were attending college but during her senior year of high school, she reached a low point in her life. While most of her friends were applying to various universities, she was not, because of financial concerns. Her high school counselor could not understand why the top student in the school was not applying to colleges.

She said, "You cannot give up. I'm going to try to find out all the scholarships I can for you and help you out, but don't give up now." She was the one that encouraged me to still apply—and see what happens later on.

The talk with her counselor gave Grace hope. Dreams that had faded because she lacked a nine-digit number were reawakened. As I listened to her story, I felt and embraced her agony. I was inspired to look at both our lives and to acknowledge how, in spite of coming from different places, growing up in different environments, and having different customs and languages, we shared something special—a very unique hope.

Grace as a child. *Courtesy of Grace Lee.*

We empathized with each other because we were engaged in the same struggle.

Grace had high hopes of attending UC Berkeley, but she could not afford the tuition and living expenses. Instead she chose UCLA so that she could live at home, and her parents could help with expenses. She commutes up to four hours every day. According to her, commuting has affected her social life. Grace has not met any other undocumented Asian students at UCLA, but she assures me that "there are plenty." I asked about the barriers she has encountered as an undocumented student.

Most of my friends are U.S. citizens. They have grants, financial aid . . . They don't have to pay for tuition . . . Some of my other friends are so rich, they say, "How much is tuition? I don't even know. My parents pay

Grace feels that her **immigration** status has led her to **establish** an important life goal: **helping** others.

for it." And whenever I hear that comment, it just hurts so much. They don't have to do anything . . . and I have to work crazy hours [to] pay for tuition, and study at the same time.

I understood, and we cried together. Yet we saw our hope grow stronger, united in one purpose. Above all the challenges, fears, and tears, Grace has been able to persist and hopes to graduate in 2008. She wants to pursue graduate studies in the field of education. Grace hopes that everything will be resolved with her immigration paperwork so she can "work for high school students and help any undocumented student or any minority student that needs my help." Although being an undocumented immigrant student has been a hardship, Grace feels that her immigration status has led her to establish an important life goal: helping others. In her own words, if she had not been undocumented, she would be "so much different."

I would be easygoing, not knowing what to do with my life. I don't know what I would be doing . . . wasting my time going clubbing, drinking, wasting money. But because I am [undocumented], I have my goals and my dream that I want to help others.

Although her parents feel pain every time they see her struggle, she comforts them by saying that she does not regret anything and that she has "learned so much." Someday, she says, "all struggles will be paid off."

The lives of students like Grace—the 65,000 undocumented students who graduate from high schools annually nationwide—will change radically if the Dream Act is signed into law. The Dream Act would provide a path to citizenship for undocumented students like Grace. If the Dream Act is enacted, she and thousands of other students will not only feel visible but also be able to contribute economically by working in their respective fields. Grace's long and unique journey has shown me that it's possible to see strength in weakness and that humans have an incredible ability to cope. She is truly an amazing Grace.

I.
I am the backbone
An equal to any
The chant at the end of the day

I am the caresser of voluptuous earth
Her and I become one
The hands that pluck and pick
to satisfy your hunger

I am the tender callus
The naked wind
The new tongue

Flesh seeking peace

I am the silent lip
The gaze that shouts

II.
Like a lonely violin
Reciting the dew of our forehead
I ignite the internal breath
Letting loose the burning vortex

Who I am
What I am
It is what your eyes do not perceive

An absent smile
River of solitude
Insurgent fist
Under the silky shadows

Listen when I speak
A simple voice
A broken voice
A tortured voice
Unfolding silence

A raped motherland
A ride on the train
at the cost of
One leg
One arm

Shattered bodies
Burned down bodies
Cut bodies
Undocumented bodies

I am an oral book
And the result of your apathy

III.
Undocumented bodies
Dehydrated bodies
Broken voices

Cochineal insects
Spread like butter
On the sidewalk of memory

Clashing spaces
Shouldering time

I plead
I plead
Cry soul of mine
Cry soul of mine

Cry...
for it's cold as Dante's hell
where demons sing
about being strong, being demons.

Cry soul of mine
Cry soul of mine

Cry...

Mario at fast. *Photograph by Jessica Chou.*

fighting another war

Erika Perez

Erika interviewed and profiled Mario Escobar. Although Mario's childhood was filled with tragedy, his resilience has led to success as an artist, a student, and an activist in the United States.

Mario Escobar was born on January 19, 1978, in El Salvador. When he was four years old, his mother left him to move to the United States. Mario's childhood was deeply affected by the social upheaval that was taking place in his hometown. In the 1980s, the government of El Salvador was at war with a guerrilla group of communists and leftists known as the Farabundo Marti National Liberation Front. The presence of slaughtered, sometimes headless bodies lying on the street was common in El Salvador.

One day as Mario and his father walked to the fishermen's union, they passed a crowd of people standing next to a military truck. As they walked over to see what was happening, Mario's father, Angel Ebaristo Escobar, grabbed his son and placed his little head against his chest as tears began to fall from his cheeks. Lying on the floor were Mario's two cousins and his grandmother, who had been brutally killed. "You become numb," were the words Mario used to describe his experience with death. "That's the only word I can think of." Mario described this graphic scene as one that he internalized: "Growing up was very difficult as a kid, having to witness

fierce combat, the gruesome atrocities . . . It was so ugly that I will tell you this much: death became something normal. You would look at a dead body and . . . pretty much, it was normal."

When Mario turned eight, he was hit with the news that his father had been killed. It was a horrible death, by lethal injection. At the young age of eleven, Mario ran away from home and picked up a weapon. Having studied Marxist theory, he decided to join the revolution and fight with the people who were facing the social injustices in his country. The tragedy continued: Mario was soon kidnapped. As soon as Mario's mother heard about his kidnapping, she returned to El Salvador and discovered that he had been released. She brought Mario back with her to the United States, only to return him a year later to El Salvador while she settled in the United States.

In 1993 at the age of fifteen, Mario decided to head to the United States on his own, traveling by train. During the trip, he was beaten several times and barely escaped being raped. After arriving in the United States, he began working as a gardener

Growing up was very **difficult** as a kid, having to witness fierce combat, the gruesome **atrocities** . . . It was so ugly that I will tell you this much: **death** became something **normal.**

and enrolled himself at Jefferson High School. At that time, the campaign to pass Proposition 187 was underway. The unfairness of the measure, which was designed to deny education, medical services, and other social services to anyone who was undocumented, impassioned Mario. His childhood experiences empowered him to organize many of the high school walkouts protesting against the passage of the proposition. He had moved, he said, from "one civil war to another, only this time without the bullets."

Mario's experiences led him to become an activist and an agent of positive social change. He educated himself about social injustice and was inspired to get involved with his community. Soon after the passage of AB 540, Mario enrolled in a community college and then transferred to UCLA, where he took on a double major in literature and Spanish. The transition to a four-year college was not easy. Mario had become a father while in community college, and he was burdened with paying tuition out of his pocket because his legal status made him ineligible for

When people think of academics, they generally picture books and lecture halls. My understanding of academics goes beyond the lecture halls. It involves what we usually read in the books—real-life experiences. I was born in El Salvador during the early period of the Salvadoran civil war; thus, I can say that my academic experience began at the age of five when I witnessed my grandmother's limbs smeared on the pavement. Next to her were my two cousins and two other victims unknown to me. At six, my twenty-year-old mother had fled the country for fear of persecution. At nine, my father had been killed for his involvement in the civil war. At eleven, I held in my hands an M-16 and was told to shoot anything that interferes with the struggle. At twelve, I was kidnapped and held captive for eleven months. In 1993 I traveled by myself across Guatemala and Mexico so that I could be with my mother. While traveling through Mexico, I saw how people risk their lives just to get to the USA. I remember seeing an old man lose his legs for trying to catch a free ride on the cargo trains. In 1993 I arrived in the United States, adopted a new culture, and learned English in one year. I enrolled in Jefferson High School in South Central Los Angeles, which was another battle zone. Witnessing shootings among gangs in 1993, I felt I was still living through a civil war. In 1996 my mother's lack of understanding and family financial obligations forced me to drop out of high school. In 1998 I decided to attend Los Angeles Trade Tech Community College but unfortunately as an undocumented student, it was hard to come up with the money to pay for my tuition, which forced me to drop out. However, I never gave up. In 2001 I returned to LA Trade Tech. In 2003 I earned my AA in science and liberal arts. That same year, I earned my GED. In 2003 I applied to the UC system and was accepted by UCLA, Cal Berkeley, and UC Riverside. It is 2007, and I am graduating with departmental honors with a dual degree in literature and Chicano studies. I will be starting my master's this fall at ASU. Although this may be seen as the end of a struggle, I can only say that the struggle does not end when one earns a degree. On the contrary, it is merely the beginning of an even bigger struggle.

Spoken word. *By Mario Escobar.*

financial aid and the majority of scholarships. Mario said that his therapy during this time was his pen. He identified himself as a poet and said that writing is like "erasing the bruises."

In his art and his way of life, Mario evidences a deep concern for the well-being of the community. He questions the way the system is set up, and he believes in equality for all people. He shows his love for his country by gaining knowledge and becoming an active citizen. He believes that salaries and educational opportunities should be more equitable for those who work hard and contribute to the economy. He believes that people have the power to make a difference if they get involved.

Mario said that Americans need to open the doors to higher education. Everyone has the right to an education, he added, and when that right is denied, the state contradicts its claim of democracy. Why must undocumented students go through the educational process only to be denied the opportunity to participate in the workforce after they graduate? Some change has to occur.

Mario believes that there are two types of democratic freedom. One is mental freedom. He argued that "when you don't have the information to know your surroundings, you're mentally restrained." The second is physical freedom—when you are allowed to go where you please. Mario noted that one can lead to the other: without knowing what to do mentally, you become physically restrained; you don't know where to go. He believes that although education does not grant you all the freedom you need, it does grant you the freedom that you need to survive in this world.

When asked for his opinion on the immigration debate, Mario explained that we need to give legal status to the immigrants that are in this country and to improve conditions in the countries where they come from. After all, as his story illustrates, it is the economic and political environments that lead people to leave their countries. He added that we need more politicians like Senator Gilbert Cedillo, who truly care about the well-being of people, especially people who are undocumented and in need of a political voice. He believes that there are a lot of "cookie cutters" in the world of politics—those who care only about climbing up the political ladder and forget about the people whose lives are affected by policy and laws.

Mario said that those who have experienced struggles similar to his should ask themselves some philosophical questions: "What is the purpose of life? What is it that you, as an individual, aim at? . . . Do you want to do something just because society tells you what to do? What is it that you aim at?"

Mario's aim is social justice and equality. He also has a personal theory about responsibility. He claims that there are

Mario with Senator Gilbert Cedillo. *Courtesy of IDEAS at UCLA.*

two types of responsibility. One requires you to fulfill duties that you are told to be responsible for, such as taking out the trash. The other requires you to do things you ought to do. For instance, being responsible means being accountable for your own actions and not responding to a harm with retribution, which perpetuates the cycle. We must not continue harmful patterns, he noted. Each of us is responsible for thinking about others as well as ourselves. A person needs to weigh the pros and cons of every situation. Mario stated that his goal is not to reach a utopian society; rather, what matters is that we *try* to reach a utopian society: "In the trajectory of wanting to reach utopia, something good is going to come out of it."

Mario has proven to be a warrior against adversity, and he continues to lead the way for undocumented students. He has published one book and has another on the way. He has started his own publishing company because there are too many voices "that need to be heard." He believes that we are living in a time of "information warfare." We need more oral histories, he stated, and we must develop new theories. He said that the struggle for equality is linked to the spread of new information.

His role is to contribute information by publishing his writing. He would like his publishing company to grow, not to gain a lot of money but to disseminate information. He would like to publish children's books that touch on immigrant issues such as AB 540. The need to educate others is his priority.

On May 1, 2007, during the rally in support of undocumented immigrants at MacArthur Park, Mario was struck, both figuratively and literally, by police violence. He filmed the incident and expressed frustration with the police officers who shot rubber bullets at the marchers: "I thought they were real bullets. They sounded like real bullets. I felt a hot sting on my upper chest . . . I saw a guy in front of me fall to the ground, and he screamed."

Mario's perseverance ultimately carried him to a major milestone. In the spring of 2007, after years of deportation hearings and just weeks before he graduated from UCLA, Mario was finally granted political asylum by the United States government. Mario is now attending graduate school at Arizona State University on a full scholarship. He is determined to influence coming generations about social justice and equality through his art.

Painting of a half-American and half-Pilipino flag, titled Struggle. *By John Carlo.*

I was going to go on **vacation**,
a vacation that would fill my life
with **hardships**
and struggles.

a downward spiral
John Carlo

In this firsthand account of John's emigration from the Philippines, the story becomes intertwined with unanswered questions about his father and untold family secrets. Although this is a real account of an undocumented student's life, a pseudonym has been used to protect the identity of the author.

At six years old, I unexpectedly caught pneumonia and was hospitalized. I was dragged down an endless, fluorescent hallway, crying furiously as I saw my mother's figure diminish. Under bright lights, they strapped me down, and I could no longer fight. It was time for me to face the four-inch needle. This is one of the last memories I have of being in my home, Quezon City in the Philippines. Months later I flew in a small charter plane to the Visayan province of Capiz to say goodbye to my grandmother and the rest of my family. I was going to go on vacation, a vacation that would fill my life with hardships and struggles.

I clung to my mother as I boarded the Cathay Pacific airliner and immediately asked the flight attendant for my child pack, which included playing cards and a coloring book. During the flight, my mother informed me that I was going to go to school in the United States. The first question that came out of my mouth was, "What if I don't know English?" My mother smiled and said, "You are speaking English." She instructed me to practice the cursive lessons that my teacher in the Philippines had given me, and she began to teach me how to multiply. After the thirteen-hour flight, we landed in sunny Los Angeles, the home of my favorite cartoon character, Mickey Mouse.

My father arrived a couple of weeks later to join me and my mother at our quaint, one-bedroom apartment in West Hollywood. I dreaded going with my mother to Beverly Hills, where she went from boutique to boutique shopping for designer clothes, but I enjoyed riding the Metro bus to the shopping mall. I also enjoyed playing the motorcycle game in the arcade and admiring the adorable puppies in the pet store. Everything about Los Angeles amazed me but after a short period of time, the glamour and beauty began to fade away. My father abruptly left us, and my mother began to fabricate various excuses to appease my curiosity. We moved out of our apartment and into a two-bedroom apartment with my Aunt May and her family.

Aunt May had a Caucasian husband whose personality clashed with my mother's. When relations between them worsened, my mother and I were forced to move out of the apartment. We stayed briefly at my Uncle Boy's apartment before my mother decided to move from Los Angeles to Daly City, which is fifteen minutes outside of San Francisco. The shuffling from apartment to apartment characterized the beginnings of my life in the United States. My mother and I had no stability, and I didn't understand why we were in the United States. I incessantly asked my mother questions about where my father was and when we were going back to the Philippines, but she always diverted them through lies that I believed every time.

These lies about my father, as well as excuses about why we had left the Philippines, were commonplace throughout my adolescence. They slowly began to ruin my relationship with my mother. I longed to learn the truth, but to pry it out of my mother was impossible. As an Asian American studies and political science major, I have had to trace and analyze my family history multiple times. I interviewed my mother and

This mother and child represent the bond between John and his mother. *Photograph by Jessica Chou.*

my younger cousin, a recent immigrant to the United States, and I analyzed my family's migration pattern in relation to U.S. immigration polices, all in order to piece together the struggles and hardships that my family still experiences today.

When I last questioned my mother about what motivated her to move to this country, she immediately responded, "Didn't I do this before?" I asked about her motivation for immigration, and she responded that she had felt that America offered an opportunity that the Philippines could not. This "opportunity" that attracted my mother to the United States was not typical of the opportunities that many immigrants seek when they come to the United States. Part of my mother's decision to come to the United States was based on the adulterous relationship that she had with my father. I was a bastard, the product of a secret relationship. My father's legal wife had found out about my mother and me, and she had made my father promise to never see us again. My father secretly continued to visit us, but his wife's suspicion caused him and my mother to plan a marriage in Hong Kong. This plan failed, and both decided that it was best to escape the *chis mis* ("gossip," in Tagalog) that was growing among their peers by moving to the United States. What was difficult for both of them was the contradiction between their love for me and the judgment of those who categorized what they had done as wrong. The grief that this caused my mother forced her to leave her life in the Philippines.

All this information was given to me by my relatives. It was never conveyed to me by my mother. In my interview with my mother conducted over the phone, she tried to steer away from the truth once again by stating that part of the reason for our immigration was educational opportunity for me. This was true, but it is clearly not the entire truth. My mother is silent about her motivation for coming to America. It is

When my **grandmother** passed away . . . there was no way we could have **gone** to the Philippines . . . I was still **undocumented**.

a subject she never chooses to talk about at the dinner table. Despite my attempts to pry the truth out of her, she replies with the same fabrications.

In the Philippines, my father was a successful attorney, and my mother worked at a bank and ran a used-car business. Overall both my parents were financially stable, and we lived a privileged life. Before leaving the Philippines, my mom sold the home that we lived in as well as plots of land that my father had given her, so that she would have sufficient funds to support us. After my father left us in Los Angeles, he continued to support me and my mother by depositing funds into my mother's account in the Philippines. My mother would then have the money wire-transferred whenever she needed more to pay for rent and expenses. For the first two years of our lives here in the United States, while we moved back and forth, this money is what my mother relied on. Family friends never took it upon themselves to help my mother because they assumed that she was wealthy and had a lot of money to spend. Many people began to take advantage of her.

I asked my mother if she thought she had been taken advantage of during our first couple of years in the United States. She paused for a moment and replied, "No, I was only trying to help other people who did not have enough money, but they always tried to pay me back." My mother was very naive and failed to recognize the intent of peers who borrowed money from her. As an optimistic immigrant, my mother thought that the people to whom she lent money would help us down the road. She eventually learned the harsh reality that her peers were only trying to gain economic prosperity for themselves.

When my mother and I first came to the United States, we were on a temporary visa that allowed us to visit for a period of six months. As our visas were about to expire, my mother became frantic and did not know what to do. She told me that my aunt, who lived in Texas, recommended an agency that would sponsor my mom for residency after she worked for the agency for a certain period of time. The downside was that she would be paid the minimum wage, which was around $4.25 at the time. My mother saw this as the only means possible to make a living in the United States, and thus she did secretarial work at this agency for three years. "It was a very simple job," she explained. "The only thing that I did not like about working was that I was not used to working long hours. In the Philippines, I was used to working four to six hours during the day and getting home in time for an afternoon nap. Part of our lives in the Philippines was much easier and comfortable because we had servants that were able to help me cook and take care of you."

On the days that my mother worked, she would tell me to walk straight home from school, which was ten minutes away from our apartment, and to not answer the door. My mother knew that one was not allowed to leave children by themselves without any adult supervision. She wanted me to be responsible and do my homework before she got home so that she would be able to check it for me. There were times when I wanted to stay and play with my friends after school ended, but my mom would always check on me with a phone call during one of her fifteen-minute breaks. "I couldn't afford a baby-sitter, which is why I had to leave you alone," she explained.

The challenges my mother encountered in the workplace were alleviated because she spoke English and because she understood the language of her bosses and coworkers; she was able to communicate with them effectively and engage in conversations. My mother shared with me

around 7:00 a.m. and not return until 8:00 p.m. because of how far she had to travel. During her interview, my mother talked about how tired she always was when she came back home because of how long she had to stay in traffic. My mother felt that the work she did was demeaning, especially because she was used to living her life with maids at her side. "At times I hated doing housework and scrubbing the floor, but I did it, or else I would get fired. However, my bosses would always treat me with respect, and the children I took care of were adorable."

Being a single mother was a tough job for my mother. There were so many days when she was exhausted but had no choice

After accepting **UCLA's** offer to enroll . . . they **blocked** the aid they had offered after finding out that I was still an **undocumented** student.

an incident in which one of her coworkers called her "paranoid." She did not know what he meant and was not able to respond to his comment. Later that day, she asked her friend from work what *paranoid* meant and when she found out, she felt very offended and saddened that someone would describe her in that way. She felt uncomfortable at work after that incident, and she soon left the agency.

My mother did not complete the time that the agency required to sponsor an individual for permanent residency, which caused a great dilemma. She had to find menial jobs that were paid under the table. The sector that my mother turned to was child care. Throughout my elementary school and middle school, my mother was a nanny for various children all over the Bay Area. She would leave

other than to go to work. The money that my father was sending was not enough to cover our studio apartment, and my mother and I had to move from apartment to apartment. The constant upheaval left us jaded and pessimistic about life. On top of our everyday financial problems, when I was in middle school, my mother and I realized that it would be very difficult to afford college. My mother decided to go back to the first agency that she worked for in order to attain legal status for both of us.

The most difficult period occurred during the spring of 1999. An aunt in the Philippines was told that my dad had died, but she was unable to confirm any of the gossip she heard because of the lack of communication with my father's family. Because she didn't know whether my father was still alive, my mother informed me that he had cancer and was very sick. I did not know the truth until one of my father's closest confidants, who lived in the Bay Area, came to our apartment and told me that my father was dead. I could not believe it. A father I never really knew . . . dead? So many emotions ran through me, but all I could do was run to my bed and cry throughout the night. "Can I go to his funeral?" I asked my mom the next day. "No, you can't, because they already cremated him," replied my mother.

A couple of months after my father's death, my grandmother passed away as well. This death was very difficult for me and my mother. There was no way we could have gone to the Philippines during this time, no matter how much we longed to. My mother was still in the process of attaining her permanent residency, and I was still undocumented. My mother wept occasionally, and I repeatedly broke down in school. We were both physically weak, and our status as undocumented immigrants only made matters worse. My mother even contemplated going back to the Philippines permanently, but she knew that it would be difficult for us to return. Despite

having no initial motivation to reap the economic opportunities here in the United States, my mom saw that there were educational opportunities for me, and she did not want me to lose an opportunity to succeed.

High school came, and I began to help my mom by working at a local department store. By this time, the INS had granted me a social security number, but there was a restriction at the bottom of my social security card that said, "This is only for working purposes." I enjoyed working because it allowed for me to earn my own money and help my mother with groceries and other expenses. I was also trying to save for college application and SAT fees.

When applying for colleges in my senior year, my mother told me to apply for financial aid. She said that my status would most likely be adjusted to permanent residency before the end of the school year. This did not occur, and although I was accepted to multiple UCs and private schools out of state, I could not afford to attend without financial aid. After accepting UCLA's offer to enroll in the fall of 2003, I encountered many problems with the financial aid office because they

John's strong academic background was motivated by his goal of earning a degree. *Photograph by Jessica Chou.*

blocked the aid they had offered after finding out that I was still an undocumented student. Because of AB 540, however, I qualified for in-state tuition.

The absence of financial aid almost forced me to stay in the Bay Area and halt my educational endeavors. Luckily my father left me a portion of money in his will and despite having the amount reduced because I was not considered a legitimate son, it was enough to pay for my first quarter at UCLA. My mother also asked one of her family friends to help us take out a loan. My first year of college at UCLA was filled with uncertainty; my mother would call me every night and talk about her financial troubles. I worked at the student store to alleviate some of the costs of school, but it was still very difficult to make ends meet. My mother said that finding the funds to help me get through the first year of college was one of the greatest obstacles we had faced since arriving in the United States. She had to move from our studio apartment and decided to rent a room in someone's house to save money to help support me.

Before my first year of college ended, my mother and I were granted permanent residency, and the restriction on my social security card was taken away. This accomplishment was long awaited, and both my mother and I were ecstatic when we got the news. I was able to apply for financial aid for the following year, and it was approved. My mother was able to find a more stable job at a post office, a place where she receives medical and dental benefits. Though I have to take out college loans, I am very appreciative of the fact that I have the opportunity to do so. Becoming permanent residents has taken away part of the burden and struggle that my mother and I have experienced, but part of the pain that it caused is still vivid.

Throughout her interview, my mom was very hesitant to answer questions about being undocumented. This may be because this type of situation is taboo in Filipino culture, largely because so many Filipino women become successful nurses in the United States. Many American Filipinos do not realize that the undocumented exist within their community and that many of them need help in breaking the stigmas attached to their legal status.

There were many pauses throughout my mother's interview, as she silently contemplated whether she was going to disclose certain information to me. I still feel that I do not know all the reasons my mother came to the United States. The only true stories that I have heard are secondhand. This unknown aspect of my past created a rift between my mother and me during my adolescence but as a young adult, I have learned to respect my mother's silence on certain issues and disregard any ill feelings I have toward her. Her silence implies that she did not want to deal with the gossip and the pain that her relationship with my father caused. As an undocumented worker, my mother worked many menial jobs in order to support us, and she has struggled to adjust to certain aspects of American culture.

Attaining permanent residency has been a long and arduous process for my mother and me. We have experienced deaths and many other hardships that have helped create a bond between us that enables us to understand each other's problems. Fear of authority, financial burdens, and cultural boundaries are just a few of the experiences we had as new immigrants to the United States. There were times during the immigration process when we were ready to give up and go back to the Philippines, but the perseverance of my mother has carried us through to this point. The celebration of my graduation this past June not only marks my attainment of a degree but also represents my struggles and successes attending UCLA.

When friends asked him about his immigration **status**, he lied, telling them that it was **pending** . . .

Nicolas in front of UCLA Kerckoff Building. *Photograph by Gisela M. Ramos.*

Secretly, he knew his status would **never** "clear."

pedagogy of a student activist

Fabiola Inzunza

Fabiola interviewed Nicolas Cervantes for this oral history. A dedicated student advocate who is deeply involved with his community, Nicolas has a promising yet uncertain future. Although this is a real account of an undocumented student's life, a pseudonym has been used to protect the identity of the person profiled.

Nicolas was born in 1985 in Buenos Aires, Argentina, into a middle-class family. He grew up in a stable house-hold; his father was an accountant for an international logistics firm based in the Bahamas and Sweden, and his mother ran a kindergarten from her home. Life for Nicolas was an adventure. As a child, he took long bike rides to neighboring cities, where he met new people, and he discovered the world through the books that he loved to read. He was surrounded by the people he loved the most. Nicolas was an outstanding student, earning high grades from his teachers and respect from his peers. This was the life Nicolas knew. It changed forever, however, as economic and legal factors intersected in a most unfavorable way.

Argentina's old labor laws, combined with an economic recession, began to affect Nicolas's father in the 1990s. During his early adolescence, Nicolas discovered that his father had lost his job. Nicolas explained that it was more beneficial for a company in Argentina to hire young college grad-uates who had no family because their bonuses were far smaller. Older employ-ees often found themselves training their young successors. At around the same time, his mother also lost her job. With no valid license to run the kindergarten, she was ordered to cease the program. She then took a job at a food market owned by Nicolas's uncle but even there, her hours were cut because of the recession.

Nicolas's dad applied for over one hundred jobs, for most of which he was vastly over-qualified. He applied overseas, including in Spain and the United States, and he finally heard from a company in California. This company told him that he was a great applicant and that if he were in the United States, he would most likely be hired. This played a great role in his father's decision to migrate to the United States.

Nicolas's dad left on a tourist visa, with the intention of coming back soon. Upon arriv-ing in the United States, he found himself in a compromising situation: he could not work legally in the United States without a valid social security number. He was confused, as he had seen many foreigners work in Argentina without legal problems. With no other source of income, he was forced to take a job at a popular wholesale market in Garden Grove, California.

Time passed and his visa expired. Pressure from home to return to his family forced him to make a drastic decision: his whole family would have to migrate to the United States for their own survival—they would never make it in Argentina. Economic recession had ushered in political turmoil, and the country's overall instability left little to return to. Nicolas's mom protested, but the family had no choice. Nicolas had just completed eighth grade when he left Argentina. He didn't have the chance to say goodbye to anyone he knew, leaving behind childhood friends that he may never see again. The plan was to stay for about two years until his father was financially established once more. Their stay turned into a decade and is now most definitely a permanent one.

able to advance through all the beginners' classes, and he soon mastered the English language. His grades began to improve dramatically.

Nicolas quickly took a path toward higher education. He achieved good grades and became very involved in his church and sports. He was resolved to attend community college because it was the most affordable option. When friends asked him about his immigration status, he lied, telling them that it was pending and that when it "cleared," he would attend a university. Secretly he knew his status would never "clear."

Because his friends were so heavily involved in school and academics, he found

Nicolas had just **completed** eighth grade when he left Argentina. He didn't have the **chance** to say **goodbye** to anyone he knew . . .

Anaheim, California, became their new home. They took refuge in the church, where they were able to meet many other South Americans, particularly Argentineans. Nicolas began to befriend fellow churchgoers. At school his grades were below average because he was just beginning to learn the English language. At home family life was difficult because his mother, who suffers from bipolar disorder, had fallen into a major depression shortly after arriving in the United States.

When it became evident that their stay would be permanent, the goals that their parents were pursuing soon turned into pushing for a better life for their children. Nicolas began to try harder in school, while his father took on a few jobs to support the family. Within a month, Nicolas was

out about a summer program that offered high-school seniors, regardless of immigration status, the opportunity to stay at a local university campus for a week and experience college life. The goal of the program was for participants to decide to further their academic endeavors by pursuing higher education. It was there that a counselor told him that under a new law, AB 540, he could attend a university without paying out-of-state tuition. The news was both relieving and inspiring to Nicolas—he would, after all, be able to receive a college education. His parents, however, still worried about being able to fund it.

Nicolas applied to UCLA, UC Santa Barbara, and UC Irvine and was accepted to all. As acceptance letters began to arrive, he began to apply for scholarships. Nicolas

EDUCATION IS A RIGHT!

Silk Painting: Education is a Right. *By Miriam Delgado.*
I am currently a student at the University of California, Davis. This piece was inspired after fasting for seven days in San Francisco. The work was designed to be a poster. I decided that the theme would be the Dream Act. Sixty-five thousand students graduate from high school every year, but many of them do not know that they are able to attend a California Community College, California State University, or the University of California.

knew that he would need a lot of financial help to attend a university, so he planned to attend a community college and transfer, a path often taken by undocumented students. Soon, however, he received a phone call from a member of IDEAS (Improving Dreams, Equality, Access, and Success) a support group for undocumented students at UCLA, urging him to attend the Academic Advancement Program's (AAP's) Scholars' Day, a day in which all incoming underrepresented youth would be introduced to the university and all the opportunities that are available to them. At this event, IDEAS hosted a reception exclusively for students who might be undocumented. Here Nicolas met fellow classmates who were in similar situations. This made him decide that UCLA was the place where he would fit in most comfortably.

Freshman year proved to be very difficult for Nicolas. With not enough private scholarship money, he was able to pay only for tuition. Housing was expensive, and the commute from Anaheim was hours long. He attempted to be actively involved with IDEAS, but he was also trying to handle a job and a loaded schedule of classes. The following year, he earned a merit-based private scholarship that paid for his housing, and his involvement in school increased tenfold. He soon became the advocacy chair for IDEAS, organizing lobbying events and various other campaigns in which he advocated for the undocumented student population. He was a member of the UCLA College Honors Program and an AAP research fellow. He participated in intramural soccer, and he got involved with UCLA radio as a dj. By hosting his own radio show, he was able to create an open forum for issues that concern his community and to provide comic relief for his friends.

Now in his third year at UCLA, Nicolas is project director for the IDEAS AB 540 Project. In this role, he advises IDEAS volunteers as they organize workshops at high school and community colleges across the county. At these workshops, volunteers distribute information regarding laws, such as AB 540, and pending immigration legislation, such as the California Dream Act. Since Nicolas began working with IDEAS, over sixty more undocumented students have been able to enroll at UCLA. Nicolas also spearheaded the kickoff campaign for the federal DREAM Act in February 2006 at UCLA. He delivered a powerful speech about the plight of undocumented students, in which he addressed the need to push politics aside and place education first as a strategy for greater educational equality for all.

Nicolas was also elected as chair of the Community Programs Office Student Association, an entity that is dedicated to making sure that the administrators of projects, such as the AB 540 Project, are properly trained and represented to the administration. In addition he has worked with the Fees and Financial Aid Campaign for the Undergraduate Student Association Council, dealing with issues such as the lack of affordability in the UC system.

Nicolas is uncertain about his plans after he graduates from UCLA. His undocumented status will not allow him to work legally in the United States, so he will have to figure out alternative means to enter the American workforce. One year from now, he will be worried about completing the classes he needs to receive his degree at UCLA but five years from now, he will still be worried about finding a job. He wants to pursue a career in the United States, the country where he grew up and where he has cultivated most of his dreams, goals, and aspirations. His plans involve going to the place where he can make the most difference.

He may not be able legally to work where he wishes, but informally he has been working with the community of undocumented immigrants his whole life. Nicolas is very much a citizen of this society. He is one of a pool of undocumented students who are high school valedictorians, class presidents, leaders in community service projects, tutors, and mentors. They are students who have decided to take their fate into their own hands and fight for an equal chance for opportunity in the United States, a country to which they have already made substantial contributions.

The story of Nicolas can be multiplied a thousand times. Many immigrants are pushed out of their native countries for an array of reasons, including economic recessions and wars. The United States is a country that takes pride in its immigrant foundations. It should not leave its immigrants in a legal limbo. Nicolas's future should not be in jeopardy, considering all that he has done for his community and will continue to do. We need legislators to take action on this urgent matter, as it may be the only way students like Nicolas can truly and fully contribute to the country that they now call home.

I believe my mother's **experience** mirrors the experiences of many immigrants who have come to the United States, led by

Scrapbook page. *By Veronica Valdez.*

the **fairy tales** that exist about the **country**. Unfortunately many immigrants have realized that these stories are only **fantasies**.

walking across the stage
Veronica Valdez

Veronica, a recent graduate of UCLA, reflects on her experience as an undocumented student and the uncertainty her future holds. Although this is a real account of an undocumented student's life, a pseudonym has been used to protect the identity of the author.

I bought my graduation robe three weeks before I graduated from UCLA. As I paid for my robe, I reminisced about how far I had come in my endeavors to succeed. Yet I could focus only on the fact that my life was now more uncertain than ever. My undocumented status has left me in a marginalized state where, even as a college graduate, the direction of my life is in limbo. I have achieved one component of the American dream: a great education. Nevertheless, I am left without opportunities for jobs in which I can use my degree—a degree that took all my perseverance to achieve, following a path that began over eighteen years ago.

My parents' decision to come to the United States in the late 1980s forever changed their lives as well as mine. From the point of our arrival as undocumented immigrants—my mother as a twenty-one-year-old and me as a four-year-old—our lives have been full of struggle and uncertainty.

It was an early Thursday morning when my mother and I got on the road to leave Mexico for the United States. My mother took only what she believed was necessary. We were headed to the border, specifically to Tijuana, where we would meet a friend of my father's who would get us across the U.S.-Mexico border. When we finally arrived in Los Angeles, my mother was relieved to finally be with my father. I do not remember reuniting with my father or crossing the border, but my mother said that I was very happy. I had cried a lot when my father first left.

My mother gave birth to my younger sister in 1991 and with a new child in the home, the need for more money became a pressing issue. My mother did not have a lot of work experience in Mexico; she worked only one job before coming to America. At the age of thirteen, her parents took her out of school and put her to work so that she could contribute to her family's household income. She worked in a restaurant until she was sixteen, and then she left her job after she met my father. She was married and had a child by the age of seventeen.

It was very complicated for my mother to find a job in the United States because of her undocumented status, which prevented her from just applying at any business with a "Help Wanted" sign. Additionally she did

It was very hard to **realize** that even though I felt like a young **American** and had been educated entirely in this nation, my **immigration** status **limited** my options and ultimately how I could live my **life**.

not know English and was unsure of where to go to learn English. She found her first jobs through friends in our apartment building and at the parent center at my elementary school. My mother's first jobs were in sales—from Mary Kay to Avon and then to Tupperware—my mom sold it all. Eventually she met a woman who worked with an agency that places workers in factories. Since 1997 my mother has worked in factories, ranging from clothing factories to packaging factories. In her current job, she packs beauty products into boxes. My mother wakes up every morning at 5:30 to go to her job in the packaging factory. Since she cannot legally get a license in the state of California, my mother takes the bus. She is too scared of being pulled over and possibly going to jail or even being deported, to drive.

For my mother, the concept of working has always been something you have to do, as opposed to an opportunity to make a difference in the world or to find fulfillment. Every day my mother comes home from work exhausted, wondering whether she will have her job the next day. She has no health benefits. Being undocumented has definitely made her position in the workforce an uncertain, frightening place to be. She has changed jobs several times because the factories have closed down, and she was advised at certain locations not to come in to work or to leave early

because immigration services were going to come. Seeing my mother go through these experiences and feeling her fear of the workplace has been a major push for me to attain my college degree.

My history in the United States began at the age of four when I was brought across the border. It has been full of both difficulties and joy. Throughout my childhood and now as an adult, I have considered the United States my home. My K-12 education was in the Los Angeles public schools. Despite the fact that I have lived in this country almost all my life, legalization has not been possible because of the complete lack of immigration legislation that addresses the needs of people like myself.

Growing up I did not have any friends who were undocumented, and I was unaware of my immigration status until I was fifteen. When I was fifteen, I decided it was time to get a job because my parents did not have a lot of money, and I wanted to buy things for myself. It was at this time that my parents notified me that I could not get a job because I had not been born in this country. From that point on, my view of what my life would be like completely changed. This knowledge made it very difficult for me to face the real world. My work experiences have varied, but most have been "under the table." I got my first job in a bakery when I was eighteen. It was the worst job I ever had. They paid me below the minimum wage, and I did not have any benefits. The work at the bakery was very hard. Being the cashier was the least of my worries; I also washed dishes, mopped the floor, cleaned the bathroom, baked the bread. I worked long hours. I had to wake up every morning before sunrise to work, and then I attended class late at night, only to come home to do class assignments. I worked very hard in school and earned good grades, but I felt humiliated. I had always had aspirations of becoming a professor, not mopping floors for low wages. I only worked at the bakery for a month before I quit. It was very hard to realize that even though I felt like a young American and had been educated entirely in this nation, my immigration status limited my options and ultimately how I could live my life.

My second job was as a waitress in a Mexican restaurant, where I worked for almost two years. At that restaurant I earned the money I needed to pay my college tuition. I worked full-time, six days a week, and simultaneously maintained my status as a full-time student. As my college education progressed, it became too difficult to hold a full-time job and maintain high grades, so I left my job. From that moment on, I have been earning money from jobs such as babysitting, washing dogs, and transcribing. I grew up seeing how hard my parents worked for the few things they have, and I wanted a better life for me and for them.

My immigration status has been a huge factor in my life in the United States. It has brought many challenges, including the inability to obtain financial aid, grants, or scholarships, to receive a valid state-issued ID or license, or to have job opportunities that match my educational level. These obstacles have contributed to my family's life of poverty. The feeling of constant uncertainty has affected me, yet I have overcome almost all the obstacles that have come my way. I learned the English language, and I have helped my family. I have paid for my college tuition, and I am obtaining the education I always desired at the university of my dreams, UCLA.

My mother has also overcome many of the challenges she has faced in the United

Veronica in a campaign poster. *By Andrew Laming.*

States. She attended English classes that were offered in the middle school I attended, and she bought tapes and videos to improve her English language skills. She found a job that has provided steady income for the last ten years. My mother has matured and given her children the motivation and advice necessary for them to succeed.

We have not been able to change our undocumented status even though we arrived in this country almost eighteen years ago. The Dream Act would allow me to change my undocumented status, opening up a path that would lead to citizenship. As beneficial as the Dream Act would be for undocumented students, we need comprehensive immigration reform that will change the legal status of millions of U.S. residents.

When I asked my mother if she would have done anything differently in terms of coming to America, she said, "Yes, I would have tried to enter the country legally, to try to find the opportunity to come legally." When I asked why she did not try to enter the country legally from the beginning, she said, "Because when the people go from here to over there, they tell you that here you earn a lot of money, that it is very easy, and they tell you of a country that is very pretty and different than what it really is. And because I did not think. I was young and did not have the maturity. I did not even know what to expect. Simply, I followed your father." I believe my mother's experience mirrors the experiences of many immigrants who have come to the United States, led by the fairy tales that exist about the country. Unfortunately many immigrants have realized that these stories are only fantasies.

My mother has not seen her mother or much of the rest of her family in almost eighteen years. With no legal way of leaving and then reentering the country, traveling to Mexico has been out of the question for years. My mother never thought she would live and raise her children in California Yet going to live once more in Mexico is not a possibility. She feels her home is where her children are, and her children consider the United States their home. My mother and I, and many other undocumented immigrants, have faced challenges every day in our attempt to create a better life for our families.

I consider myself American. My friends, boyfriend, family, hopes, and dreams are in this country. Thus, I work in every way I can, in every movement I can, to be recognized by the nation I have lived in for so long.

I Run. *By Laura Marcela.*

I run and run, it doesn't wait for me, late to class I guess.

I turn around and I see a woman waiting, her beautiful brown
skin radiates in the sun, she reminds me of my mother.

Her thick navy blue sweater warms her, and she is now ready
to face her day as a commodity. She will go to a wonderful
mansion in the hills of Beverly to take care of children that are
not her own.

Her children go to school in some of the most underprivileged
schools in the L.A. area, they come home to an empty house,
no parents allowed in the home 'til the immigrant working
quota has been met, 'til they have done their service to a
country who labels them as aliens.

The woman looks at me, her eyes look tired and sad, but there
is something in them that shows perseverance and strength,
the perseverance to continue the struggle of the minority
masses, the strength to leave her children behind and raise the
children of the privileged, the perseverance to stand strong and
face her daily chores at the hands of the elite, the strength to
survive for her family's future.

But will this perseverance and strength be sufficient?
Will her dreams of having college-educated children come true?
Or will these dreams be crushed by the same country she so
strongly believes will provide better opportunities, a country
who turns the other cheek and ignores the children of
immigrants, a country who does not listen to the urgent call
for resources and aid for students everywhere, who will tell her
that her struggles will be fruitless, who will dim the light of
her hope?

The bus arrives, I find a seat in the back and think, maybe late
to class is not so bad.

I am a UCLA graduate with a BA in sociology and anthropology, interested in pursuing a career in cultural anthropology. Due to financial circumstances and legal status, I needed to commute to UCLA using public transportation. On my trips to and from campus, I would encounter different people in the bus. I was especially captivated by the women who where going to work from impoverished neighborhoods in East L.A. to West L.A. These women inspired me to write the spoken-word piece. As an AB 540 student, I not only experienced first-hand the struggles of being an immigrant but I have seen it in the eyes of the Latino community that surrounds me. May the struggle and the resilience of our people continue to grow.

My father felt a
responsibility
to America . . . The military
did not help soldiers advance,

Gregory is an activist. *Courtesy of University of California Students Association.*

and they were **fighting**
in wars they did not necessarily
understand.

a legacy of colonization
Gregory Allan Cendana

In this account, Gregory explores his family's history of cultural conflict and cultural denial as well as what it means to be a Pilipino American fighting for the rights of undocumented students in the United States.

Like many other immigrants, my parents moved to the United States to find "greener pastures" and better opportunities, in the hope of advancing in life and realizing the American dream. As part of the immigration wave that followed the passage of the Immigration Act of 1965, my parents have been deeply impacted by U.S. colonization in the Philippines and the pressure to assimilate into U.S. culture and politics. These ideologies particularly influenced my parents' education and later, their experiences in America. Although my sister and I were born in the United States, I can relate to the immigrant struggle because I have directly experienced its effect on my family. My parents' lives as immigrants and ours as second-generation Pilipino Americans have laid the foundation for my immigrant-rights activism and my critique of U.S. imperial power both on communities in the U.S. and abroad.

America's colonization of the Philippines extended directly into the country's education system, a system that holds Western forms of learning far above all other knowledge. The educational curriculum was designed to teach Pilipino students about America's history rather than their own, and that is exactly what my parents learned. They were not aware of Pilipino history before colonization. In addition the education system stressed the importance of speaking fluent, unaccented English. American history courses were taught in English, which helped perpetuate the use of English in the classroom and at home. The influence of English continues to be prevalent and is still the primary language in the Philippines today.

Though my mother grew up in Manila, and Tagalog was her first language, she soon realized that she had to learn English to succeed in the Philippines. When she looked for work in America, she ended up working as a teller at Bank of America. She explained that "in the Philippines, you have to have a college degree to get a decent job, even a job as a teller, like the one I have here in the U.S. In America this job only requires a high school degree." For my mother, being educated in the Philippines was advantageous because her knowledge of English made her a viable candidate for jobs once she immigrated to America.

My father had a different experience. He was born in Japan on a U.S. Navy base, and he lived there for three years. From there he moved to Seattle, where his father was stationed. When he turned eleven years old, he moved to the Philippines,

With my **privilege** as a U.S. citizen, I feel . . . a responsibility to **advocate** for the **rights** of those who aren't as lucky as I am.

and then he returned to the United States at the age of nineteen to enlist in the military. Though much of his education was in America, his experiences in the air force have definitely been a major influence on his decisions and his view of his experiences in Japan, America, and the Philippines. My personal experiences coupled with my research and interest in learning about my community's history have shaped the way I understand the impact of colonization on my family's immigration and how I share a common history with many other immigrants in the U.S. today.

Similar stories of not only fellow Pilipinos but many diverse immigrant communities have moved me to become an activist advocating for the rights of immigrants and people of color. At UCLA I helped found the Student Activist Project (SAP), a social-justice internship that, through reflection and action, helps guide students toward understanding the roots of many social problems and how such oppressive structures of power are sustained. SAP teaches youth leaders the skills needed to affect social change and offers students the opportunity to put into practice what they learn. By participating in social-justice organizations, they become more committed students and community leaders.

Through this type of work, I have become intimately involved in defending the rights of undocumented students who are unable to regularize their immigration status. So many of the AB 540 students' family stories I hear resonate with my parents' belief

that if you work hard and serve this country, somehow your loyalty will be rewarded. Whether it is the household worker or day laborer toiling long hours, or my father working for the U.S. Air Force expecting to receive the same benefits as other enlisted men; immigrants hope that the U.S. will recognize and acknowledge their contributions. Still, millions of hard-working immigrants live in the shadows. Neither comprehensive immigration reform nor the Dream Act has been passed to reward these students and workers for their years of dedication.

As the former internal vice president and progressive presidential candidate for UCLA's student government, I authored and cosponsored a resolution in support of undocumented students. In addition I have brought legislative issues regarding the rights of undocumented students to the attention of the University of California Student Association (UCSA) and the United States Student Association (USSA). In turn these organizations have made the California and federal Dream Acts legislative priorities.

"I worked. And I worked hard," my father said. "Grandpa joined the navy because he wanted to serve his country. I joined the air force to do the same." I speculate that there was an additional, underlying reason. As described by Ronald Takaki in *A History of Asian Americans* (1998), fighting in World War II gave Pilipinos the chance to show themselves to America as "soldiers of democracy"—as "men, not houseboys." My father wanted to prove that he was an

Participants at the May Day Rally hold flags that represent their countries, May 1, 2006, MacArthur Park. *Courtesy of IDEAS at UCLA.*

American and assimilate into the culture. Fighting in the war was the only way he could do that. My father felt a responsibility to America and to follow in the steps of my grandfather. In reality the military did not help soldiers advance, and they were fighting in wars they did not necessarily understand. My father continued to serve in the military for many years after the war ended, but he saw little benefit. As a result of his colonized education, he rationalized America's irresponsible treatment of the Pilipino people and linked my resistance to joining the military to a lack of allegiance to America.

Through my studies at UCLA, my family's history, and my activist work with community-based organizations and undocumented-student groups across California, I have learned about and experienced the legacy of American colonization. In particular I have witnessed the

toll this legacy has taken on my friends and family. Though not their fault, this legacy is evident in my parent's unquestioning pro-U.S. political views, their lack of understanding about Pilipino history, and their disinterest in preserving Pilipino culture within our family. This legacy is also apparent when Central American undocumented students tell me about their families' sagas fleeing American-sponsored and American-supported wars that devastated their countries. I have also become aware of the immense disparities and failed trade agreements that exist between neighboring Mexico and the U.S. that have forced so many of my classmates' families to migrate in search of economic survival.

Growing up in America has offered me liberties that my parents did not and will not have. Students of my generation are free to choose what we want to study. If I want to study mechanical engineering or Asian American studies or business economics at UCLA, I can do so. With our experiences in higher education, we are better able to direct our careers, and we have a better understanding of our economic and political opportunities. The importance of education was instilled in me by my parents, pushing my generation to be more conscious of world history and more critical of U.S. colonization. This view has led me to be troubled by my parents' lack of understanding and often unwillingness to examine the past. It has also led me to support the struggles of undocumented students who are fighting to be recognized as valuable contributors to this society, despite the unwillingness of a nation to recognize them.

The question now becomes: what should my generation do with our knowledge? If we acknowledge that we are living in a different place and time with a different political climate and economy, we must also recognize the privileges that we have acquired as second-generation immigrants. With these privileges come the challenge and responsibility to be active and to educate and provide avenues for political consciousness regarding the key issues of our day. It is for this reason that I have chosen to walk side by side with my undocumented student peers. It is for this reason that I struggle to understand my parents, their generation, and the systems that shaped who they are. As critical as I am of these experiences, I will use them to empower myself and to ensure that future generations of young activists do not receive the miseducation that has affected my family and many young people when it comes to the history of U.S. immigration and colonialism.

With my privilege as a U.S. citizen, I feel that it is necessary and a responsibility to advocate for the rights of those who aren't as lucky as I am. By keeping the history of my family and the continuous struggle of AB 540 and other undocumented students in mind, I am reminded each day that without collective, community support across all races, ethnicities, genders, sexualities, abilities, and immigrant status, social change and equality will not be achieved.

My Secret Identity

My Secret Identity once consumed and tortured
every ounce of my being.

Like in the prisons of Abu Ghraib and Guantanamo Bay,
My secret identity was humiliated, ravaged, and beaten.

My secret identity was imprisoned and forced to
gruesomely watch its own raping.
Its own destruction.

My secret identity became a target for hatred.
It became a monstrous alien, something subhuman,
something that could be disposed of.

Unarmed and unprepared to protect myself as a child,
I was forced to watch as my secret identity sustained
blow after blow after blow.

I wanted to defend it but I could not.
I did not know how, I did not know what to do, what to say.

I wanted to scream and yell at the images and headlines in the
media to stop!
My secret identity was not a Criminal! It was not illegal!

As I grew and entered high school my secret identity was
mentally terrorized, psychologically tormented,
emotionally terrified, linguistically attacked

And to my soul …

Hope was loss,
Hope was shackled in chains,
Hope was destroyed,
Hope was murdered,
Hope was oppressed,
Hope was not a word,
Hope did not exist …

Today education and concientizacion have begun
to heal my secret identity.
To nurture it, to rebuild it, to restore it from the
mental damage of annihilative attacks.

The lacerations are closing, but the invisible scars are still there.
Recovery is near but the revolution to free my
secret identity still wages on.

Uniting with other fellow revolutionaries and their secret identities,
We vociferously march in collective numbers,
to liberate ourselves from hopelessness.

My secret identity will no longer be a secret or
source of imprisonment.
Equipped with a revolutionary mind and a relentless
commitment of self-sacrifice for La Causa
Today to my soul …

Hope is not lost,
Hope is found,
Hope is not in chains,
Hope is shattering chains,
Hope does exist,
Hope is alive and breathing,
Hope is a word by which inner strength flows out of me.
Hope is what feeds the compassion in my life to change society.

Antonio's first home in America. Photograph by Jessica Chou.

out of my hands
Antonio Alvarez

In this personal history, Antonio shares his memories of crossing the Mexican border with his mother and his thoughts about the ways in which anti-immigration legislation has cast a permanent shadow on his academic career and family life. Although this is a real account of an undocumented student's life, a pseudonym has been used to protect the identity of the author.

As I ran downstairs from the third floor, I looked forward to playing with the other children living in our apartment building. Some of my friends were playing with *trompos* (a top spun with yarn, like a dreidel), others with marbles, and some of the girls were jumping rope. I noticed that one of the children had a water gun very similar to mine. I approached the boy, took a closer look at the toy, and realized that it actually was mine. I asked the boy why he had taken my water gun and told him that he needed to return it. He said, "No, your mother sold it to me because you guys are leaving. You guys are moving away, somewhere else." This was when I first knew that I was going to the United States. I was four years old.

My father, Antonio, said that he decided to go to the United States "to be able to have a better life, a better future, in being able to realize our dreams, the American dream." Similarly my mother, Alida, "did not see a future for us in Mexico" and viewed the United States as the answer to our problems. During the 1980s, Mexico underwent a major economic crisis, leaving my father without a stable job to support our family. The instinct to survive led both of my parents to view immigration as their only option. My father left in mid-1988, and the rest of the family—me, my mother, two-year-old brother Isai, and eight-month-old sister Alida—left in late December 1989.

The plan was for my father to work in the United States and send money back home to support us and hopefully to accumulate enough to start up our own business. My mother grew impatient in Mexico when my father did not return however. She

Antonio as a child. *Courtesy of Antonio Alvarez.*

believed he needed to see his children. She decided to migrate with the entire family to the United States without giving prior notice to my father. To finance our trip north, my mother resorted to selling our belongings; thus, my toy gun contributed toward the trip.

From what I remember of the trip, it started at a motel in Tijuana, where we stayed for two nights before crossing the border early in the morning. I remember my mother making a phone call from Tijuana to my father, telling him that we were on our way to Los Angeles. There were about fifteen or twenty people crossing that day. The coyotes—the men we paid to help us cross the border—were extremely scared to take us, telling my mother, "Lady, we have never crossed children before. You know this is very risky." My mom told them that she knew and acknowledged the risk factor but said we were going to cross. I just thought it was the way everyone went to the United States: walking and running for hours as quietly as possible through rough terrain.

We started the actual walking part of the trip at a dump yard and continued on until the dump yard ended and turned into scrubby hills. From that point on, we ran, jogged, and walked for hours. I remember at one point, my shoes became dirty from stepping in the mud, and I said, "Oh no, my shoes are dirty," and everyone

in the group loudly said "shhhhh" for fear of detection. The border patrol agents were inside vehicles that gave them an elevated view of the area and allowed them to more easily spot any immigrants. From that moment on, I realized that I had to stay as quiet as possible throughout the trip. Some moments my mother vividly remembers from the trip include crossing the I-5 freeway, and the other migrants telling my mother, "Come on, lady, run, run! Come on, run," and me telling her, "Come on, mami, run! Run so you don't get left behind, run, hurry, hurry mami!" She also remembers how I held my little brother's hand for part of the trip to help him along the way and how a young immigrant couple helped my mother by carrying my baby sister for most of the trip.

After traveling for several hours on foot, we arrived at a cabin in the hills with other crossing immigrants. At this point, I was extremely hungry. Inside the cabin, as my family rested, I spotted three or four over-toasted, cold tortillas—hard, like tostadas—that someone had left. I ate one and took another one for my little brother. Though they did not taste good, my brother and I finished them out of hunger. We left the cabin and got inside a car that the coyote had obtained. With about three other immigrants in the car, the coyote drove us to Los Angeles, where my father was waiting at a bus stop. My mother was the first to see him standing

I just thought it was the way **everyone** went to the United States: walking and **running** for hours as quietly as possible through **rough terrain**.

on the street. As I looked at him for the first time in over a year, all I wanted was to run up and hug him. We arrived in Los Angeles a few days before Christmas.

My parents' plan was not to permanently settle in the United States; however, as time passed, they decided to stay. One of our goals became, and continues to be, to adjust our residential status from undocumented to documented permanent residents. My father filled out numerous applications to adjust his residential status, and the process was long and arduous. He began in 1992, but due to a mistake of addresses when we changed residences, and a long waiting list, it took my father about fourteen years to adjust his status. He obtained a work permit in 2003 and finally his permanent residency in 2006. Now he has petitioned for permanent residency for me, my siblings, and my mother, but the waiting list is so long—a lifetime for us.

Along with our residential status, anti-immigrant laws have shaped our lives in the United States. My parents said that the laws that have affected us most severely include California's Proposition 187, which was approved by voters in 1994. My mother believed it was not fair to keep children out of public schools and to keep them from receiving medical treatment. We were surprised at how much support the proposition gained and that an overwhelming majority of Californians voted for it. My mother told me that I would probably not be able to attend school any more if my undocumented status was reported by anyone on the school staff. Though the proposition passed, it was struck down as unconstitutional by the courts, and I continued to attend school.

I remember the 1996 driver's license legislation's passing and going into effect, because my dad was worried to death by it. He was mortified because at that time and up until 2006, he had been working

As a child, Antonio met his father at this bus stop in Los Angeles. *Courtesy of Antonio Alvarez.*

two jobs—one of them as a pizza delivery worker for different pizza chains, which required a valid driver's license. It was hard watching how much stress he had because he knew renewing his driver's license would be impossible, since the new law prohibited undocumented immigrants from receiving licenses or renewing them. By the time my father had to renew his license, however, he had received his work permit. It allowed him to renew his driver's license without any legal trouble.

Though I remember these laws as severe obstacles for our family's livelihood, legislation affecting higher education opportunities for undocumented students stand out in my memory most prominently. I realized that I was an immigrant and that something was not right during the Proposition 187 campaign but until I reached high school, I did not understand that my future would be seriously limited. During my freshman year, I discovered that I could not obtain a license because I was undocumented, and during my junior year, I realized the hardships I would face upon entering college. I had achieved almost a 4.0 grade point average up until my sophomore year, but when I learned that I could not receive any federal or state financing to attend a four-year university, I became demoralized, and my grades suffered from it. I thought there was no point to continuing to work so hard in high school if attending a community college—where my high school grades would be irrelevant—was my only option.

My outlook changed a few months before high school graduation. I talked to one of my teachers who was once an undocumented immigrant student but is now a permanent resident. He told me about AB 540 and explained that it would allow me to pay in-state tuition at UC, CSU, and community college. Though I was accepted to CSU Los Angeles and CSU Fullerton, he recommended I first attend a community college for its affordability, complete my first two years there, save money, and then transfer to a four-year university.

I took his advice and enrolled at East Los Angeles College (ELAC) in the summer of 2003 and quickly followed this by searching for a job. As a result of my undocumented status, I could not work anywhere I wanted and was limited to low-wage jobs that did not require identification or background checks. I was hired at a market, where I worked over thirty hours a week. I now had a goal. My plan at ELAC was to work and go to school and then to transfer to a CSU because the UCs and private schools were too expensive and required longer commutes. Though it was a good plan, it saddened me because my ideal dream from years before—ever since I had visited the UCLA campus during an elementary school field trip—had been to attend a top university.

I enjoyed the schooling I received at ELAC, and I flourished. I took sociology classes and fell in love with the subject. It was then that I realized that I wanted a career in helping others, specifically individuals whose voices were muted in society. Impressed by my work, both my sociology and English professors told me I needed to include a UC in my future. When I finally did apply to transfer, I was accepted to every university I applied to: USC, UC San Diego, UC Berkeley, and UCLA. I decided to attend UCLA, where I struggle for the thousands of dollars to finance my education. I will graduate with a degree in sociology and Chicana/o studies.

Being undocumented has been a way of life for me, my family, and millions of others. When I apply for jobs that I know I am overqualified for but that do not include background checks, I experience strong feelings of detachment and frustration, followed by hints of helplessness. I work these jobs to pay for a college experience that does not include semesters abroad and living in a dorm and other experiences that "normal" students have. I hope that by sharing some of my family's history and experiences—as undocumented immigrants, undocumented workers, undocumented students, undocumented people, and second-class human beings—I can help produce an emphatic and humanistic approach to immigration that vigorously rejects the notion that a human can be illegal.

Graduation for many
of my friends isn't
a **right of passage** to
becoming a responsible adult.

Tam working on a documentary. *Courtesy of Stephanie Solis.*

Rather it is the last **phase**
in which they can feel
a sense of **belonging**
as an American.

testimony of tam tran

Tam Tran

Tam Tran is a courageous undocumented student, who has testified twice before Congress. A twenty-four-year-old graduate of the University of California, Los Angeles, Tam immigrated to America at the age of six. For years Tam's family, refugees from Vietnam, have fought for American citizenship. However, major obstacles in the immigration system have prevented this reality from happening. Below is Tam's testimony before the House Judiciary Committee's Subcommittee on Immigration, Citizenship, Refugees, Border Security and International Law. Following Tam's testimony are two articles that were published about her life in the Los Angeles Times *and* USA Today.

I hate filling out forms, especially the ones that limit me to checking off boxes for categories I don't even identify with. Place of birth? Germany. But I'm not German. Ethnicity? I'm Vietnamese, but I've never been to Vietnam. However, these forms never ask me where I was raised or educated. I was born in Germany, my parents are Vietnamese, but I have been American-raised and -educated for the past eighteen years.

My parents escaped the Vietnam War as boat people and were rescued by the German navy. In Vietnam my mother had to drop out of middle school to help support her family as a street vendor. My father was a bit luckier; he was college educated, but the value of his education has diminished in this country due to his inability to speak English fluently.

They lived in Germany as refugees and during that time, I was born. My family came to the United States when I was six to reunite with relatives who fled to California because, after all, this was America. It is extremely difficult to win a political-asylum case, but my parents took the chance because they truly believed they were asylees of a country they no longer considered home and which also posed a threat to their lives. Despite this, they lost the case. The immigration court ordered us deported to Germany. However, when we spoke to the German consulate, they told us, "We don't want you. You're not German." Germany does not grant birthright citizenship so on application forms, when I come across the question that asks for my citizenship, I rebelliously mark "other" and write in "the world."

But the truth is, I am culturally an American and more specifically, I consider myself a Southern Californian. I grew up watching Speed Racer and Mighty Mouse every Saturday morning. But as of right now, my national identity is not American and even though I can't be removed from American soil, I cannot become an American unless legislation changes.

In December I graduated with a bachelor's degree in American literature and culture with Latin, departmental, and college honors from UCLA. I thought, finally, all these years of working multiple jobs and applying to countless scholarships, all while taking more than fifteen units every quarter, were going to pay off. And it did seem to be paying off. I found a job right away in my field as a full-time film editor and videographer with a documentary project at UCLA. I also applied to graduate school and was accepted to a PhD program in cultural studies. I was awarded a department fellowship and the minority fellowship, but the challenges I faced as an undocumented college student began to surface once again.

Except the difference this time is I am twenty-four years old. I suppose this means I'm an adult. I also have a college degree. I guess this also means I'm an educated adult. But for a fact, I know that this means I do have responsibilities to the society I live in. I have the desire and also the ability and skills to help my community by being an academic researcher and socially conscious video documentarian, but I'll have to wait before I can become an accountable member of society. I recently declined the offer to the PhD program because even with these two fellowships, I don't have the money to cover the $50,000 tuition and living expenses. I'll have to wait before I can really grow up. But that's okay, because when you're in my situation you have to learn to, or are forced to, make compromises.

With an adult job, I can save up for graduate school next year. Or at least that's what I thought. Three days ago, the day before I boarded my flight to DC, I was informed that it would be my last day at work. My work permit was expired, and I won't be able to continue working until I receive a new one. Every year I must apply for a renewal, but never have I received it on time. This means every year around this month, I lose the job that I have. But

that's okay. Because I've been used to this—to losing things I have worked hard for, not just this job, but also the value of my college degree and the American identity I once possessed as a child.

This is my first time in Washington, DC, and the privilege of being able to speak today truly exemplifies the minimal state I always feel like I'm in. I am lucky because I do have a government ID that allowed me to board the plane here to share my story and give to the thousands of other undocumented students who cannot. But I know that when I return home tonight, I'll become marginalized once again. At the moment, I can't work legally even though I do have some legal status. I also know that the job I'm going to look for when I get back isn't the one I'll want to have. The job I'll want, because it makes use of my college degree, will be out of my hands. Without the DREAM Act, I have no prospect of becoming what I've always considered myself to be—an American.

But for some of my friends, who could only be here today through a blurred face in a video, they have other fears too. They can't be here because they are afraid of being deported from the country they grew up in and call home. There is also the fear of the unknown after graduation, a fear that is uniquely different from other students. Graduation for many of my friends isn't a right of passage to becoming a responsible adult. Rather it is the last phase in which they can feel a sense of belonging as an American. As an American university student, my friends feel a part of an American community—where they are living out the American dream among their peers. But after graduation, they will be left behind by their American friends, as my friends are without the prospect of obtaining jobs that will utilize the degrees they've earned; my friends will become just undocumented immigrants.

Undocumented. *By Mariana D. Zamboni.*

Uncertainty is the foundation of our existence.

No one knows why

Disciples of knowledge would be

Ostracized.

Can't they see the

Unlimited resources we bring?

Miles of hard work and

Ethical concerns but...

No one will fully understand

The pain that we carry inside.

Endless tears may wash away our fears but the...

Daily struggle is the only thing that's real.

Mariana D. Zamboni was born in Guatemala and migrated to Los Angeles at the age of six. She grew up in Pico Union and graduated with a degree in psychology from UCLA. She benefited from the passage of AB 540 in California and will be starting a master's degree in education at Harvard University in Fall 2007. She hopes to continue to fight for accessibility to higher education for all immigrant students.

I wrote this poem on one of those days when hopelessness takes over, and I began wondering, why do I submit myself to such agony. Sometimes I felt that little by little, a piece inside of me would die, and I felt tired of working hard and of being motivated when in the end, I was not going to get anywhere. In those days, the only favorable solution was to quit; but faith in a better tomorrow would always settle in after tears of desolation dried.

Vietnamese Refugee Family in Limbo

Teresa Watanabe, *Los Angeles Times*

Government actions in a deportation case involving a Vietnamese refugee family in Santa Ana drew fire Thursday as political and community leaders accused immigration agents of intimidation.

Agents with the U.S. Immigration and Customs Enforcement agency last week arrested the parents and brother of Tam Tran, a 24-year-old UCLA graduate who testified before Congress about the plight of undocumented immigrant students in May. The family, detained overnight and then released under electronic monitoring, had received final deportation orders in 2001 after losing an appeal to win political asylum.

Rep. Zoe Lofgren (D-San Jose), who heads the House immigration subcommittee that called Tran as a witness, said she was concerned that the arrest would intimidate other activists into silence.

"What message does that give future witnesses—that if you give testimony to Congress, your family is arrested?" Lofgren said in an interview Thursday. "I'm very concerned. This is intimidation."

Lofgren said she planned to call a public hearing this year to scrutinize the immigration agency's actions in this and other cases.

The Asian Pacific American Legal Center in Los Angeles also criticized the arrest.

"Many in our community are scared to come out and lend their voices to the immigration debate because of actions like these," said Daniel Huang, the center's policy advocate. "The suspicion is that the administration is trying to silence the powerful advocacy going on behalf of undocumented immigrants."

Virginia Kice, the immigration agency's spokeswoman, said agents did not know about Tran's congressional testimony when they arrested her family members in an early morning raid Oct. 11. Kice said the arrest was part of the agency's stepped-up efforts to find and deport hundreds of thousands of illegal immigrants with final orders of deportation—efforts that have snared 61,000 people in four years.

"This had nothing to do with any congressional testimony," Kice said. "The bottom line is that at present these family members all have final orders of deportation, and our responsibility is to endeavor to carry out those orders."

At the moment, however, no country is willing to take the Tran family back—placing it in a legal netherworld.

Like so many other boat people, Tam Tran's parents left Vietnam in 1980, fleeing war and political persecution triggered by the family's anti-Communist activities, Tam Tran said. They were picked up by a German ship and taken to Germany, where they tried to apply for resettlement in the United States but could not locate a sponsoring relative, she said.

The family stayed for six years in Germany, where Tran and her brother, Thien, were born. In 1989, they came to the United States and applied for political asylum.

As their case worked its way through the system, the Tran family was able to obtain legal work permits and painstakingly built a life in the U.S. Tran's mother, Loc Pham, baby-sat by day and worked at a garment factory by night, eventually earning her manicurist license. Her father, Tuan Tran, worked as a security guard and now struggles as a writer.

Tran graduated cum laude in American literature from UCLA and is working at a Los Angeles nonprofit organization to earn money to pursue a doctoral degree. Her brother works as an auto mechanic.

The family bought a mobile home, pays taxes and has no criminal record, Tran said. They report every year to U.S. immigration officials to renew their work permits.

But the Trans' dreams were crushed in 2001 when the Board of Immigration Appeals rejected their asylum claim. The board found that Tuan Tran faced political persecution in Vietnam and could not be returned there—among other things, his father was an anti-Communist journalist who was imprisoned and eventually died in captivity in Vietnam. But the board ruled that the family should be deported to Germany, where they had safe haven until they voluntarily decided to leave.

Germany, however, has refused to accept the family. Because the Trans left Germany without official permission and have been gone for more than six months, their residency permit has expired and will not be reissued, according to Lars Leymann, spokesman for the German Consulate in Los Angeles.

"They therefore have no legal claim to go back to Germany," Leymann said. "It's the law. We see no reason to change our position on that."

Kice, of the immigration agency, said U.S. officials would continue to seek travel documents from Germany to send the Tran family back. Another option, she said, was to see whether the political climate had changed enough in Vietnam to allow the family to return there without fear of persecution.

Sending them back, however, could be difficult because the U.S. government still does not have a repatriation agreement with Vietnam.

Another alternative would be to find a third party to accept the family, Kice said.

Lofgren said that if Germany declines to change its position and accept the family, the Trans' asylum case could be reopened to seek permanent residency in the U.S.

"These people have been found to be refugees," said the Tran family attorney, Dan Brown of the Los Angeles-based Paul, Hastings, Janofsky & Walker LLP law firm. "They're no danger to anyone."

Tam Tran, meanwhile, said she just wants to get past the uncertainty and angst and be able to make the United States her permanent home.

"At the end of the process, we have nowhere to go," she said. "We're in a black hole."

Immigrant's Family Detained after Daughter Speaks Out

Kathy Kiely, *USA Today*

WASHINGTON—Three days after a 24-year-old college graduate spoke out on her immigration plight in USA TODAY, U.S. agents arrested her family—including her father, a Vietnamese man who once was confined to a "re-education" camp in his home country for anti-communist activities.

Rep. Zoe Lofgren, D-Calif., who chairs the House immigration subcommittee, on Tuesday accused federal officials of "witness intimidation" for staging a pre-dawn raid on the home of Tuan Ngoc Tran.

The agents arrested Tran, his wife and son, charging them with being fugitives from justice even though the family's attorneys said the Trans have been reporting to immigration officials annually to obtain work permits.

Lofgren said she believes the family was targeted because Tran's eldest child, Tam Tran, testified before Lofgren's panel earlier this spring in support of legislation that would help the children of illegal immigrants. On Oct. 8, Tam Tran was quoted in USA TODAY. Her parents and brother were taken into custody Thursday. The family was released to house arrest after Lofgren intervened.

"Would she and her family have been arrested if she hadn't spoken out?" Lofgren said of Tran, who was not at home for the raid but has been asked to report to Immigration and Customs officials next week. "I don't think so."

Kelly Nantel, a spokeswoman for U.S. Immigration and Customs Enforcement, said the Tran family's arrest "absolutely, unequivocally had nothing to do" with Tam Tran's advocacy. She said ICE agents began working on the case Sept. 28 and will now try to send the family to Germany, where the Trans lived for several years before coming to the United States. In the past, the German government refused the family's permission to return; Nantel said the U.S. government will now make an official request.

The raid marked the latest chapter in the Tran family's complex immigration odyssey. The family arrived in the USA 18 years ago from Germany, where the elder Trans ended up after the German navy rescued them at sea when they were escaping Vietnam.

Both Tam Tran and her brother, Thien, 21, were born in Germany, but they have lived in the USA since they were young. Tam Tran received a bachelor's degree with honors in American literature and culture in December from UCLA.

She has lobbied for the DREAM Act, which would give children of illegal immigrants a chance to obtain citizenship if they earn

Tam, *right*, and members of the U.S. Congress, May 18, 2007, Washington, DC. *Courtesy of the Office of Congresswoman Lucille Roybal-Allard.*

a high school degree and complete two years of postsecondary education or two years of military service.

In 2001, the Board of Immigration Appeals said the Tran family could not be deported to Vietnam because Tam's father had been persecuted there for his political beliefs. The board left open the possibility that the family could be sent to Germany, but German authorities wouldn't give them a visa.

Nantel said there are more than 324,000 people living in the USA who have been ordered deported but who can't be sent away because no country will accept them. It's ICE's job to find ways "to effect the judge's order," she said.

Bo Cooper, a Washington-based immigration attorney who this week agreed to take the Tran family's case free of charge, said he's puzzled that "the U.S. government would go and try to deport someone who doesn't have a criminal record and who has been given formal protection" because of his treatment at the hands of the Vietnamese government.

Nantel acknowledged the Tran family had been reporting to immigration officials regularly. Asked why they were arrested and charged with being fugitives, she said agents "did not understand the complexity of the case." She said ICE agents removed the family's electronic ankle bracelets Tuesday.

Part III

TAKING ACTION

Students rally at the May Day March, May 1, 2007, Los Angeles. *Courtesy of Susan Malgarejo.*

The Inv s bles

¡Gracias Firebaugh!

Students rally support for DREAM

While the immigration debate rages on in the U.S. Congress, undocumented students have continued to fight for their dream—the American dream. They have taken action to bring attention to the Dream Act and to the marginalized state in which they find themselves, using outlets that range from newspaper articles to radio shows to congressional hearings. Undocumented students have also participated in marches, rallies, and mock graduations. One of their latest attempts to bring attention to their plight was a hunger strike. They have reached out to elected officials and have employed every method possible to bring forth the positive change they wish to have in their lives. The Dream Act would give outstanding, high-achieving, undocumented students the opportunity to finally be recognized by American society. This is imperative because undocumented students are a vital and positive force in American society. If the Dream Act is passed, these students will no longer live in an uncertain, marginalized state. Despite the opposition that undocumented students have faced, they have proven to be strong. They will continue to take action until just legislation is passed.

TAKING ACTION
Artwork by Gabriela Madera and Wendell Pascual

Background photo: Students listen to speeches by undocumented students at the IDEAS Mock Graduation Rally, February 28, 2007, UCLA.

The Inv s bles

The students in UCLA's undocumented immigrant club struggle for an education others take for granted, getting by without financial aid, traditional IDs, even a place to live. They're smart and determined. But do they have a future here?

By Douglas McGray

Me siento extra

único país que c

THE REAL SOLUTION

Making the Dream a Reality

Saturday, May 19th 2007
Ackerman Grand Ballroom, UCLA

the DREAM was ... Congress four years ago and would low students who were b e Unit ts to b me legal citizens even if ey parents are undocumented, said arielena Hincapie, a staff attorney nd director of pro ngeles National enter, a legal insti w-income immigr The bill has been cause of its contr While opponent mented immigra warded by becoming citizens, pro-

La Opinión

¡Gracias Firebaugh!

CALIFORNIA
MIGUEL CARVENTE

Acabo de enterarme hace algunas horas, por medio de un mensaje electrónico que me mandó mi profesor de Estudios Chicanos que el venerable Marco Antonio Firebaugh había muerto. Mi sorpresa se convirtió en incredulidad ante el mensaje, hasta pensé sería el 1 de abril—el día que aquí llamamos *April Fools Day*, o el Día de los Inocentes— y pensé llamar a mi profesor para decirle que bromas como ésas jamás se deben hacer.

Todo esto pasó por mi mente, pues sólo hace un mes había tenido el honor de conversar con Marco A. Firebaugh. En esa ocasión se mostró como un hombre lleno de vitalidad, orgulloso de sus logros cuando era legislador y ansioso de regresar a la política —para seguir ayudando a la comunidad. También se veía humilde, pues me contó que como legislador solamente trabajaba para la comunidad que lo eligió, incluyendo los que no podían votar por él.

Al llegar la tarde del 21 las noticias me informaron que en verdad había muerto el ex legislador estatal. En ese instante me sentí muy triste y surgieron estas letras porque al igual que muchas otras personas, lamenté el fallecimiento de Firebaugh. Hemos perdido a un hombre que durante su término no legislativo se preocupó por ser la voz y promover leyes que nos ayudan a los inmigrantes indocumentados, los que estamos preocupados de que nos quiten los pocos derechos que tenemos.

Mientras era legislador estatal, Firebaugh sobresalió por crear la Ley AB540, que dio las esperanzas de alcanzar una mejor vida a miles de estudiantes indocumentados en California. Esta ley, por la cual es mayormente conocido, entró en vigor en 2002 y le da la oportunidad a miles de estudiantes de continuar con sus estudios universitarios.

Esta ley permite que un estudiante indocumentado pueda calificar para pagar el mismo precio que los residentes en las inscripciones para los colegios y universidades públicas de California siempre que haya asistido a una secundaria local un mínimo de tres años.

La Ley AB540 tenía la intención de ayudar a una porción de los 50 mil a 60 mil estudiantes indocumentados que, según se estima, se graduían de la secundaria cada año. Esta ley nos brinda ayuda al hacernos elegibles a pagar las mismas colegiaturas que residentes legales y ciudadanos, en vez de aplicarnos las costosas tarifas de estudiantes fuera-de-estado que se nos imponía antes que Firebaugh creara la ley.

Quizá para algunos les pueda aparentar que esta la ley no brinda demasiada ayuda, pero esto no puede estar más lejos de lo cierto. En efecto, la Ley AB540 nos brinda una tremenda oportunidad de asistir a un colegio o universidad. Por ejemplo, mientras un ciudadano y residente legal pagan aproximadamente ocho mil dólares al año por asistir a una universidad de UC, a un estudiante indocumentado se le cobraba cerca de 30 mil. Igualmente, las colegiaturas en el sistema universitario CSU le cuestan a un residente y ciudadano alrededor de tres mil dólares al año, mientras a los estudiantes indocumentados se les cobraba cerca de 12 mil. Además, en los colegios comunitarios los residentes pagan 57 dólares por unidad, mientras a nosotros nos cobraban entre 114 dólares.

Es necesario aclarar que la Ley AB540 no sólo ayudó a los estudiantes indocumentados, sino también benefició a muchos más ciudadanos. Esto se debe a que es incluso con colegiaturas más accesibles, para muchas familias por estas cantidades Además, los cinco dólares que aprovechan la ley son aquellos que se mudaron de California, regresan con el propósito de completar sus estudios universitarios, y no desean pagar las colegiaturas de estudiantes fuera-de-estado.

Estoy triste, irónicamente, porque la Ley AB540 y otras que beneficiaron a los inmigrantes fueron una fuente de nuestra felicidad. Hoy sólo podemos especular cuánto bien pudiera haber hecho Marco A. Firebaugh como senador estatal. Todavía existen políticos que abogan por los inmigrantes, pero se nos ha ido un integrante de este grupo que ha dejado su marca como pocos.

Tuve el gran honor de conocer a Marco A. Firebaugh y me dijo algo que jamás olvidaré. Él explicó que en su vida había recibido más satisfacción en ser un oficial electo, pues ahí descubrió que ción de ayudar al prójimo, una persona es capaz de hacer una gran diferencia.

Por último quisiera decir que cada ocasión que pude encontrarme con Firebaugh siempre procuré expresarle mi gratitud. Nunca me cansé de hacerlo. Por eso quiero concluir diciendo: ¡Gracias y descansa en paz!

Miguel Carvente es estudiante de bachillerato en la Universidad de California en Los Angeles.

Left: IDEAS invitation for Making the Dream a Reality banquet. *Background photo*: Students from throughout California march to support immigrant rights on May Day, 2007, Los Angeles.

attend
college
2nd Annual
Making the Dream A Reality
Banquet
May 19, 2007
DREAM
NETWORK
DEPORTATION
from page 1
He is also frightened by the
than a decade after the end of
Help me
reach
my dream
Citizenship
Handbook
SENATOR GILBERT CEDILLO
REGISTER TO VOTE
VOTER REGISTRATION CARDS AVAILABLE HERE

Top left: IDEAS, by Carol Belisa Monte. Bottom left: Students urged people in their communities to vote. Top: Students speak out about immigration issues on KPFK radio. Bottom: Kent Wong speaks at the Hearing and Conference on Undocumented (AB 540) Students, May 19, 2007.

The school did not **release** private scholarship **funds** that were earned by undocumented students—

Students represent IDEAS. *Courtesy of IDEAS at UCLA.*

some of them were **revoked** entirely, while others were **simply** not distributed.

Improving Dreams, Equality, Access, and Success (IDEAS)

Wendy Escobar, Heidy A. Lozano, and Fabiola Inzunza

In 2003 a group of UCLA students along with advisors Jeff Cooper, Alfred Herrera, and Adolfo Bermeo created a support group for undocumented students at UCLA. Improving Dreams, Equality, Access, and Success (IDEAS) was designated to encourage, promote, and further the college education of undocumented students by providing them with academic and financial resources and a community of support. IDEAS members work together to fulfill their personal and educational goals as undocumented individuals; they are the professionals of tomorrow and the mentors needed for coming generations.

IDEAS has three components:

1. disseminating information regarding pending legislation that affects undocumented students at state and federal levels through a community service project, the IDEAS AB 540 Project;
2. recruiting incoming undocumented students and retaining the enrollment of existing members by alleviating financial burden through fund-raising efforts;
3. advocating for the rights of undocumented students at the university, state, and federal levels.

The founders of IDEAS came together because of their shared circumstances as undocumented AB 540 students. Because AB 540 was a newly implemented piece of legislation, many of them did not know until they attended the first IDEAS meeting that dozens of UCLA students qualify for in-state tuition. Members quickly decided that their first goal would be to tackle the immediate issues they face on the UCLA campus.

Many of the members' frustrations revolved around simple university procedures. For instance, many campus transactions, including visits to the school's clinic and hospital, required students to have government-issued identification or proof of a social security number, something that undocumented students could not provide. Additionally the school did not release private scholarship funds that were earned by undocumented students—some of them were revoked entirely, while others were simply not distributed. IDEAS members contacted different members of the campus community in an effort to bring attention to these problems. New liaisons were formed with administrators who worked

IDEAS invitation for Making the Dream a Reality banquet.

with IDEAS members to address the numerous concerns shared by undocumented students. These liaisons soon became crucial conduits for the dissemination of information to other UCLA students, and they were pivotal in creating networks with other campus groups.

In addition to problems with administrative procedures, it was hard to retain IDEAS members at UCLA. The economic status of undocumented students is an issue that is not completely addressed by AB 540. Although the bill did alleviate the financial burden of paying out-of-state tuition, in-state tuition is still very expensive without any financial support from the government. Thus, IDEAS members had to look for creative ways in which they could raise money for their college tuition.

IDEAS founding member and past co-chair Maria Lucia Chavez recalls one of the first humble fund-raisers: the sale of enchiladas, pan dulce, and tamales. As IDEAS member Delia Torres attests, "I can honestly say that if it were not for IDEAS, I would not have attended UCLA my freshman year." Furthermore, the fund-raisers helped the original members gain organizing experience and leadership skills, which are fully practiced now that their attempts at fund-raising have grown to large-scale banquets. All proceeds go

directly to incoming and current students who face extraordinary obstacles in paying for their books and tuition.

IDEAS was also concerned about recruitment efforts. How could they increase the number of undocumented students at UCLA and other universities? This was addressed through the formation of a community service project, the AB 540 Project. Aptly named for the law that opened the doors of higher education for many of IDEAS members, the project's mission is to find more undocumented students and to share the information and, most importantly, the resources that have enabled IDEAS member to attend UCLA. Members host workshops for high-school students, counselors, parents, and other community members at various locations. One notable workshop is the IDEAS reception, which that takes place during the UCLA Academic Advancement Program's (AAP) Annual Scholars' Day. These workshops show undocumented students who have been accepted to UCLA how to apply for scholarship money and describe real financial options for pursuing higher education.

IDEAS has been so successful in educating students that many high schools and community-based organizations now call on its members to give presentations and to attend events as guest speakers and panelists. When the AB 540 Project was established, the goal was to reach thirty high schools; that year the project ended up reaching out to sixty. This achievement proved that the distribution of information was long overdue. First-year undocumented students were able to feel a sense of community and receive guidance about their options in higher education.

The presence of IDEAS has greatly increased not only on the UCLA campus but also throughout the state and beyond. IDEAS has garnered support from many allies, including students who are not undocumented but strongly believe in the organization's efforts. These efforts have included rallies calling for the reduction of fees to make education affordable for people in economic need; a mock graduation highlighting the contradiction that undocumented students face when they receive their degrees but cannot use them to seek employment; lobbying in Sacramento for the California Dream Act; rallies and mock graduations in Washington, DC; and working with a statewide network of students in a weeklong fast in support of the federal DREAM Act. The members of IDEAS have slowly started to speak louder, and their voices are being acknowledged.

IDEAS works in collaboration with administrators, staff members, professors, departments, other campus organizations, community members, and public officials. It is important to note the diversity of these groups and how this reflects the diversity of IDEAS members, who come from a variety of ethnic and national backgrounds, demonstrating that the issue is not one-dimensional or one-sided. The number of people now involved with IDEAS promotes collective action, which will benefit a wide range of people.

The founders of IDEAS hope that the organization will continue to evolve so it can help more and more undocumented students. In the near future, the founders expect to make IDEAS a licensed, nonprofit organization; this will allow IDEAS to increase its funding through more donations. As a nonprofit, IDEAS can extend its scope and become a stronger coalition that can organize more support for its cause.

IDEAS member Marla Ramirez proudly states, "IDEAS allowed me to further develop my leadership skills and be able to demand the rights of undocumented students in higher education." Now, thanks to the AB 540 Project, more students are aware of their options and have the tools to attend college. The dissemination of information to other campuses and the expanded advocacy for legislation has increased dramatically since 2003. While fund-raising continues to grow, and more undocumented students have received the financial assistance they need to achieve a college education, the number of undocumented students at UCLA grows faster. Nonetheless, IDEAS is a success story; it has built a strong community that continues to grow.

epilogue
Angelo A. Mathay

The Immigrant Rights, Labor, and Higher Education class at UCLA strongly hopes that the personal stories collected in this book will give readers a deeper comprehension of what is at stake in the immigration debate for undocumented students. The media will continue to publish rhetoric that negatively portrays the struggle of undocumented immigrants, but one must remember that those who describe undocumented immigrants in unflattering terms are oftentimes unaware of how much the United States is dependent on them. We must make the United States change its obsolete immigration laws and end the exploitation of undocumented immigrants. In order to do so, we should all engage in the immigrant rights movement and participate in campaigns that advocate for the legalization of all undocumented immigrants and the passage of the Dream Act. The needs and the basic rights of undocumented immigrants can no longer be ignored. In solidarity we can eradicate the injustices of the past and fulfill the dream of millions of undocumented students.

"The people united will never be defeated."

Main photo: Summer 2007 UCLA Labor Center interns. *Inset photo, left*: publication team interns. *Inset photo, right*: outreach and education interns.

RESOURCE GUIDE

Hector Saldivar

LEGAL ORGANIZATIONS

Legal Aid Foundation of Los Angeles
8601 S Broadway Ave, Los Angeles CA 90003
(213) 640-3884
http://www.lafla.org

The Legal Aid Foundation of Los Angeles (LAFLA) is the frontline law firm for low-income people in Los Angeles. LAFLA is committed to promoting access to justice, strengthening communities, fighting discrimination, and effecting systemic change through representation, advocacy, and community education.

Mexican American Legal Defense and Educational Fund
634 S Spring St 11th Fl, Los Angeles CA 90014
(213) 629-2512
http://www.maldef.org

The Mexican American Legal Defense and Educational Fund (MALDEF) is a nonprofit organization that protects and promotes the civil rights of Latinos in the United States. Education is one of MALDEF's focus areas, and it is engaged in an effort to increase immigrant student access to higher education. After the passage of AB 540, MALDEF launched a statewide outreach and training campaign to inform counselors, students, educators, community-based organizations, and community members about the requirements of the law and the availability of resources to finance a higher education.

Mexican American Bar Association of Los Angeles County
714 W Olympic Blvd Ste 450, Los Angeles CA 90015
(213) 749-2889
http://www.mabalawyers.org

The Mexican American Bar Association (MABA) is one of the largest and most prominent Latino bar associations in the nation. MABA's mission is founded on the commitment to the advancement of Latinos in the legal profession and the empowerment of the Latino community through service and advocacy. MABA supports AB 540 students and offers them scholarship opportunities.

National Immigration Law Center
3435 Wilshire Blvd Ste 2850, Los Angeles CA 90010
(213) 639-3900
http://www.nilc.org

NILC develops in-depth analysis of proposed legislative and regulatory changes that advocates and policymakers rely on for accurate

Students throughout California went to Los Angeles in support of changing current immigration legislation during the May Day marches, May 1, 2007, MacArthur Park.

information. NILC disseminates timely legislative updates and alerts, creates workgroups of representatives from national advocacy organizations and community agencies, and coordinates strategic responses to policy changes. NILC strongly supports the Immigrant Student Adjustment/ DREAM Act.

Asian Pacific American Legal Center
1145 Wilshire Blvd 2nd Fl, Los Angeles CA 90017
(213) 977-7500
http://www.apalc.org

APALC's mission is to provide legal services, education, and civil rights support to positively influence and impact primarily the Asian Pacific American community. APALC is the largest Asian American civil rights organization in the country.

COMMUNITY ORGANIZATIONS

Central American Resource Center
2845 W 7th St, Los Angeles CA 90005
(213) 385-7800
http://www.carecen-la.org

CARECEN's mission is to empower Central Americans by defending human and civil rights, working for social and economic justice, and promoting cultural diversity. CARECEN has been a great supporter for AB 540 students.

Coalition for Humane Immigrant Rights of Los Angeles
2533 W Third St Ste 101, Los Angeles CA 90057
(213) 353-1333
http://www.chirla.org

CHIRLA has been at the forefront in the fight for immigrant and refugee rights in Los Angeles and across the state and nation. CHIRLA created the student committee Wise Up to win access to higher education and immigration reform for all immigrant students.

Korean Resource Center
900 S Crenshaw Blvd, Los Angeles CA 90019
(323) 937-3718
http://www.krcla.org

KRC was founded in 1983 to empower immigrant communities and people of color, particularly Korean Americans, through education, advocacy, and grassroots organizing. One of the most important goals of this organization is to advocate for the civil rights and immigrants rights of Korean Americans and to legalize undocumented students.

Salvadoran American Leadership and Educational Fund
1625 W Olympic Blvd Ste 718, Los Angeles CA 90015
(213) 480-1052
http://www.salef.org

SALEF has built education and youth programs to assist future generations to gain knowledge and skills for high school, college, and beyond. SALEF offers scholarships to students regardless of their immigration status.

STUDENT ORGANIZATIONS

Bakersfield Community College
Immigrants Determined for Education and Academic Success (IDEAS)
Email: ideas.bc@sbcglobal.net

East Los Angeles Community College
Student Advocates For Higher Education and Equality (SAHEE)
Email: elac_saheequality@yahoogroups.com

Glendale Community College
Voces Del Mañana
Email: voces_dm@yahoo.com

San Bernardino Valley Community College
MEChA de SBVC
Email: sanbernardinodream@yahoo.com

Santa Monica College
Association of Latin American Students
http://www.smc.edu/eops

Riverside Community College
MEChA
Email: rccdreamers@yahoo.com

CSU Dominguez Hills
Espiritu de Nuestro Futuro
Email: espiritudenuestrofuturo@yahoo.com

CSU Fullerton
Alliance of Students for an Equal Education (ASEE)
Email: asee_csuf@yahoo.com

CSU Los Angeles
Students United to Reach Goals in Education (SURGE)
http://www.groups.yahoo.com/group/csula_surge
Email: surge@calstatela.edu or csula_surge@yahoogroups.com

CSU Long Beach
Future Underrepresented Educated Leaders (FUEL)
Email: fuelcsulb@yahoo.com

CSU Northridge
Dreams To Be Heard
Email: dreamstobeheard@yahoo.com

CSU Pomona
Demanda Estudiantil Para La Igualdad Educacional (DEPIE)
Email: depie_calpolypomona@yahoo.groups.com

San Jose State University
Student Advocates for Higher Education (SAHE)
http://www.geocities.com/ab540students/Officers.html
Email: ab540students@yahoo.com

University of California, Berkeley
Rising Immigrant Scholars through Education (RISE)
Email: ucb_rise@yahoo.com

University of California, Davis
Improving Dreams, Equality, Access, and Success (IDEAS)
Email: ideas_ucd@yahoo.com or ucdavis_ideas@yahoo.com

University of California, Irvine
Dedication for the Realization of Education and Always Motivated for
Success (DREAMS)
Email: dreamsatuci@yahoogroups.com

University of California, Los Angeles
Improving Dreams Equality, Access, and Success (IDEAS)
http://www.studentgroups.ucla.edu/ideas
email: ideas@ucla.edu

University of California, Santa Barbara
Improving Dreams, Equality, Access, and Success (IDEAS)
Email: ideasatucsb@yahoo.com

University of California, Santa Cruz
Students Informing Now (SIN) Verguenza
Email: porlacausadelosestudiantes@yahoo.com or sin_ucsc@yahoo.com

University of California, San Diego
Migrant and Immigrant Rights Awareness at UCSD (MIRA)
Email: migrant-rights-awareness@googlegroups.com or ucsdiversity@
yahoo.com

University of Southern California
Center for Higher Education Policy Analysis (CHEPA)
http://www.usc.edu/dept/chepa